THE DIARIES & WRITINGS OF AN ALCOHOLIC MISSIONARY

"WE EXIST, AND ARE LIVING AMONG YOU..."

Boyd Walker

The Diaries & Writings of an Alcoholic Missionary:
"We Exist, and are Living Among You..."

Copyright © 2019 by KAAPU
All Rights Reserved.

Library of Congress
ID#: 1-7624502871

ISBN 978-0-578-52552-5

No part of this book may be reproduced in any form, except for the inclusion of brief quotations in reviews, without permission in writing from the author or representatives.

KAAPU Publishing
KAAPU – P.O. Box 435 – Salem, AR 72576

Facebook: Simple Truth – Boyd Walker

www.thealcoholicmissionary.com

KAAPU

In partnership with Craft Book Publishing
www.CraftBookPublishing.com

CONTENTS PAGE

ACKNOWLEDGEMENTS 7
INTRODUCTION 9
PROLOGUE 15
CHAPTER ONE 19
CHAPTER TWO 35
CHAPTER THREE 63
CHAPTER FOUR 79
CHAPTER FIVE 99
CHAPTER SIX 115
CHAPTER SEVEN 127
CHAPTER EIGHT 137
CHAPTER NINE 149
CHAPTER TEN 171
CHAPTER ELEVEN 179
CHAPTER TWELVE 205
EPILOGUE 227
TIMELINE 231
OTHER BOOKS BY THE AUTHOR 235
ABOUT THE AUTHOR 237

William, Phillip & Matthew
You were the ones most effected by the man
within these pages, and probably the most grateful
for the father that has taken his place...

&

'To the alcoholic who still suffers'.
The Sunlight of the Spirit awaits you.
There is still Time and Hope my friend, until there is not...

ACKNOWLEDGEMENTS

I would like to thank Renata Namo, Johnson Ellis, Francesca Giessmann and Chiara Gadaleta for providing the editorial readings, corrections and 'tidying-up' of some of the vocabulary, context and format of these diaries. They have spent countless hours making sure the book is relative and on-focus to both the religious and alcoholic communities we wish to reach.
The language I used to express myself in the original diaries would be offensive to some readers. However, it was how I felt, and I normally expressed my feelings 'colorfully'...
I would also like to thank the thousands who traveled with me during these years. The work you accomplished is astounding in scope. Hundreds of thousands of people have been reached with Hope and Health through your efforts. May God continue to bless each of you...

INTRODUCTION

This is the first of three books containing the **"Diaries & Writings of an Alcoholic Missionary:"**. These are the actual writings of a man who drank his way through 29 years of torturous, duplicitous life before becoming sober in 2006. He was perplexed by his own behavior involving numerous separations from his wife, elicit affairs and blackouts while in the midst of doing 'God's Work'. The diaries contain narratives added to help provide context and insight as to the author's personal circumstances at the time of the writings.

One of the greatest misconceptions of the Christian Community today is that most every negative, deviant, or otherwise unbecoming behavior, is a "sin" resulting from the absence of repentance, forgiveness and just enough faith to continue on in a more 'acceptable' manner.

This 'exclusive' belief, held by the very community self-charged with bringing hope to a lost world, has led to the exclusion of some of the neediest, desperate, most gifted human beings ever to grace this earth. The preaching of this false dogma has served to alienate the very segments of society for which Christ was known to have shown the most compassion. Alcohol falls squarely into this category of 'unresolved sin', leading to the death of both body and soul. Alcoholism is a disease, not a sin. However, *untreated alcoholism* leads to some of the most reprehensible sins known to man. This distinction, often not recognized by the well-meaning Christian Community, is important to know and understand because it is *true*.

Alcoholism is not racist or exclusive in nature. It will take root wherever 'relief' feels needed. It discriminates against no leader, person, religion, gender, sect or societal norm. It presents itself as a helper. It will insist on being the solution to all calamity, human frailty and chaos. It offers courage to the afflicted; reassurance to the fearful; hope to the hopeless and refuge to the weary. It wears the disguise of 'all things good'. As one of my fellows once described it long ago, "Alcohol gives the alcoholic wings to fly. But one day, without exception, will take away the sky...'

Alcoholism has no known cure. As with any disease of an incurable nature, remission is the best that can be hoped for. And this, *only* through the dedicated, lifelong treatment of its cause.

I drank because I *chose* to drink. No one and nothing should be blamed for it but *me*. By the time I lost the element of "choice" in the matter, thus becoming alcoholic, I was beyond human aid, with a family and a multitude of people who would follow me virtually anywhere I might lead them.

As the years accumulated, so did the painful, convicting guilt and shame that I felt. However, the only solution I could comprehend at the time, was to secretly drink more and more. More drink and sedatives were needed with the dawning of each new day. By the time I reached my bottom, I had been at the helm of one of the most effective, independent missionary organization in the Amazon Valley of Brazil, for more than 20 years.

Not fully understanding the nature and gravity of my mental, spiritual and physical state, the diary entries contain a mixture of desperation, hypocrisy, defeat, surrender and hope – even though I couldn't see or feel it, I intrinsically knew there was hope...

I was baffled by the stance of the church regarding my dilemma. I was a 'believer'. I was doing a work of the Kingdom few others were capable of doing. My church, however, believed people with my problem were just 'unrepentant sinners'; 'weak and unresolved with Christ'; 'never truly saved' at all. I knew *none* of this was true of myself. I also knew *no* help would likely come to me, or anyone like me, from this church I had looked to for reassurance and healing.

I was born in 1959, to a Southern Baptist missionary couple, appointed to Brazil, S.A. My parents were amazing human beings and did their best to raise up my brother and me in the "Way we should go". They instilled Christian values and led us each to a personal relationship in Christ.

I had no problem with anything I was taught. I just didn't get it for some reason. I remember feeling scared to trust in anything but myself. I could trust 'in theory' but not in reality as I saw and experienced it.

Although an introvert by nature, I set about making a 'splash' everywhere I landed. I'd found alcohol at the age of 14. It worked miracles in subsiding the fear and anxiety I felt deep inside. So profound was this fear that if alcohol had not 'worked it's magic', some other substance would surely have been found and embraced.

I left home at 16, determined to live in any manner necessary to survive and succeed in a world I didn't comprehend. My father paid for a ticket back to the USA and loaned me enough cash to buy an old VW and not starve in the process of getting settled somewhere.

I ended up in South Florida; rented a room in the slums (with an exposed toilet in the corner and communal, outdoor shower privileges) and started working wherever anyone would hire me. Now on my own, the more I drank the easier it became to deal with the world, and whatever there was to accomplish in or through it. To my surprise and delight, 'good things' began happening.

These early years brought relative success my way. By the age of 20, I'd partnered in several small businesses. The old VW gave way to new cars sporting fancier 'abbreviations'. My home address now included the Atlantic Ocean in the front yard and a pool in the back, neither of which I paid much attention to.

As this worldly success increased, so did my drinking, and now, drug use. My outward appearance and persona was polar opposite to the profound emptiness and conflict relentlessly feeding on my soul. Deep inside I knew the path I was on needed altering. However, faced with 'reality' and the fear of any change, I drank even more. As to the question of peace and tranquility for my life, 'oblivion' was the only answer that seemed to work.

Finally, on December 5th, 1985, during an alcoholic blackout, I suffered what was termed a 'lifestyle-induced cardiac event'. I woke up in the ICU of a hospital, having no idea where I was or how I'd come to be 45 miles from my home and businesses. Although confused, I felt no fear or panic. I remember intrinsically knowing I was finished. I could go no further; didn't want to go any further. If God would still have me, I'd let Him show the way forward.

A great weight seemed to have lifted through this 'bottom' experience. But, I *still* thought the future was largely up to me. I *still* didn't get what was truly needed for life to look and feel differently, to be what it might or could be.

In less than two years, I would drink again. Only this time, the dynamic had become far more complicated. I had embarked in doing "God's Work" by then. The level of surrender needed to affect sustainable change in my existence would continue to elude me for another 20, internally ruinous, years.

As my alcoholism progressed, so did my seeming inability to understand what was wrong with him. I'd been taught that alcoholism was a sin and had, therefore, prayed *incessantly* to be 'delivered' from the hell I had created for myself and those close to me. All of this desperate 'pleading', leading to no sustainable effect.

Finally, on October 06th, 2006, I'd reached the point of no return. I found myself in a place beyond all human aid. I knew, in every fiber of my being, that I could not continue on. Not for even another, single day. By God's Grace, I had finally reached the point that had, thus far, eluded me – a place where there was no more possibility of avoidance or denial – a point of unbridled, total surrender of all that was left of me. The Sunlight of the Spirit was finally dawning, nevermore to be darkened, one-day-at-a-time...

Through my life, writings and diaries, I desire to magnify several truths to all who have followed me through the years, and to those joining the journey now:

- Know that alcoholism is a disease that requires treatment, just like any other life-threatening illness known to man. It is birthed through fear, illusion and delusion and grows through guilt, shame and the misunderstanding of its very nature.
- *Self-knowledge is not enough* for the alcoholic to begin recovery. So, nothing one can say or do will speed up this journey and process. If an alcoholic is to survive at all, recovery must be initiated by his or her, and no one else
- A good alcoholic will go to *any* lengths to protect himself and his ability to drink, often making it hard to recognize him or he in your midst. 'Missions' and 'Pastorates' are ideal endeavors and environments to harbor people like us. It is easy to hide and protect oneself while involved in such "high callings". Few suspect our presence.
- Know that *all* alcoholics need help. Be aware, however, that *few* will seek such help, and most will die drunk. The best thing one

can do for an active alcoholic is pray God allows him to experience a tangible 'bottom' before death ends all possibilities for recovery.
- Know, without a doubt, there are leaders among you, in schools, local churches and mission fields, that are currently living lives very similar to that revealed in my Diaries. Be alert in your religious surroundings. Consider having compassions on your leaders when they fall. *All harboring such secrets will eventually fall.* Regardless of background, profession, position in life or level of 'faith', *no one* is fully immune to such things.
- If you know of an alcoholic in need, the most effective help available will be found through your local Alcoholic Hotline or that of other disease-specific, 12-step fellowships. These understand the problem and *live* in the solution.
- As the 'church' is probably the *first* place the Alcoholic left due to rejection and shame, it will likely be the *last* place he will return to. Don't rush this process. If and when the time is right, most of us do return.
- There should be *no* question regarding alcoholism being a disease. God has provided for it's treatment. He has done so though 'recovered' alcoholics. The Church needs be aware of its limitations in this realm.
- By reading and examining these Diaries, it is my prayer that both active and potential alcoholics may see *themselves* in enough of it that help will be sought.
- It is my belief that *every pastor, staff member* and *congregant* should read these diaries and be aware that *we are among you*, desperately in need of help...

PROLOGUE

The setting for these diaries is the Amazon Valley of Brazil. More specifically, on the more remote lakes and tributaries of the mighty Amazon River.

The Amazon is the largest river on earth. It boasts more than 1,100 tributaries. Seventeen of these, outsize the great Mississippi River. The Amazon is 4,000 miles long. As it passes Obidos, Amazonas, it is a staggering 600 feet deep. It's mouth stretches to more than 210 miles in width and pushes freshwater more than 200 miles into the Atlantic Ocean.

Conservatively, more than 20% of both the freshwater and oxygen of the world is attributed to this vast area. The Amazon Rainforest is among the densest and less populated of any other of its kind in the world. This is where Boyd was raised and ultimately settled for long stretches of his life. It is where he still lives and works today.

Boyd founded an independent mission organization in 1986. His primary intent in doing so was to share Christ where none others had cared to go. At the perimeter a church or denomination would end its reach, is where Boyd's organization would begin its efforts. One of the main precepts that drove Boyd in this work was to never duplicate the efforts of any other denomination. Where someone was already serving the physical and spiritual needs of a people, he would not interfere. His desire was to always go deeper into the Valley than any had gone before.

The organization worked under the belief that the "full person" should be helped. If there were sick, heal them *first*. *Then*, share the spiritual reason for having come and helped at all. Boyd's organization was the first to bring organized teams of medical, construction and evangelism from the USA to the remote areas of the Valley. The first to deal with indigenous groups. The only one today that is still active in reaching the unreached, regardless of logistical challenges or cost. The organization invested heavily in its own vessels and hospital to provide both stability and mobility for these efforts. The "logistical blueprint" Boyd established through his life and work is still followed by most other organizations that emerged over the decades.

By the time Boyd relinquished his leadership role over the organization in 2012, it had treated more than 600,000 patients; provided roughly 1,100,000 prescriptions; performed more than 300,000 surgical procedures and was known and highly regarded among the river-dwellers and numerous indigenous tribes of the Amazon Valley. All the above at no cost to the recipients.

Boyd and his organization endeavored to go deeper than anyone ever before. This required teams of volunteers willing to take risks; willing to enter harm's-way if need be; follow instructions to a 'T' and follow almost blindly in to rainforest often referred to as the 'Green Hell'.

Although all the names have been changed in order to protect the identity of those involved, Boyd wishes to commend these individuals and teams for their courage, faithfulness and dedication. Without their willingness to join these ventures, very little would have been accomplished of all that was. More than 3,000 such volunteers joined and followed Boyd throughout these years on the Amazon. Scarcely a handful knew anything of his alcoholism.

However, all were safe and secure during these ventures. Boyd was a professional and surrounded himself with sober staff at all times.

The names of towns, villages, rivers and lakes mention in these diaries, *are* real. Boyd no longer travels to many of these places. In sobriety, his desire to go 'deeper still' has intensified. He is most likely to be found on one of the minor tributaries, to a small tributary, of a major tributary to the might Amazon River itself. As a matter of fact, where he lives and travels these days is mostly uncharted or has yet to be named. He has thatched huts scattered among various clans of isolated tribesmen.

Boyd maintains contact with the outside world through his satellite communication systems. His schedule of appearances, in the USA along with varied writings and the occasional video, may be accessed via the website below. He is always willing to help an alcoholic who still suffers and *wants* such help. Otherwise, find him if you can...

www.thealcoholicmissionary.com

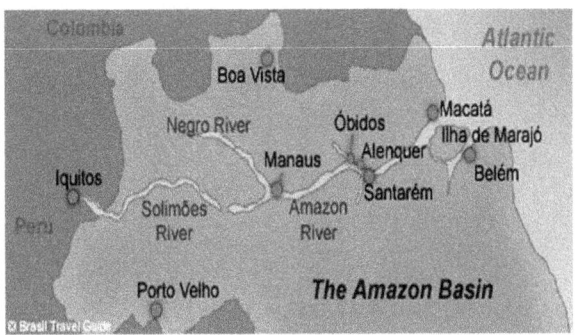

The Setting for these Diaries...

CHAPTER ONE

**Vic's ultimatum was clear:
"If you are still drinking, don't come home…"**

The selected diaries of this collection begin in March of 1999. I had just returned from the USA after a 6-month stay, working for a friend in Kansas City, while attempting to abstain from alcohol. At this point, my wife (Vic) and I had been separated for almost two years. The terms, mutually agreed upon for my return home, were that I stop drinking, stay away from other women and continue to grow the Mission Organization I had founded, 13 years prior. I had done well in these areas while I was away. But, upon my return to Brazil, the stresses of home and business were beginning to overwhelm me once more. The period of abstinence from alcohol ended just two month after I returned. One of my key responsibilities around the Organization was to visit the areas and people where our mission teams would be affecting their participation with us. These 'preparatory trips', along with 'exploratory trips' to new regions, were done ahead of time so I could put together the logistics needed to make the *teams' efforts on location as successful as humanly possible. I was recognized as 'the best there ever was' in these areas. I had literally 'written the book' that most other organizations follow to this very day. This particular trip was one of searching for me. I desperately wanted to be rid of alcohol. I, however, was clueless as to how this goal might be achieved. I had tried most everything I knew to try. None of it had provided anything close to lasting control or relief. I had hoped that a bit of exclusive, intensive time spent with 'men of God', during this particular trip, would lead to some insight that I'd somehow missed before – maybe even leading to a permanent solution of some kind. As I set out on this venture, I was hopeful…*

PREPARATORY TRIP TO THE RIVERS AND LAKES OF THE LOWER AMAZON
March 20 – March 25, 1999

March 20: It's 6:55 P.M. I'm headed out with Pastor Gilberto and his family to parts unknown. All I know is that I am here and feel my very life may depend on the events of these next days.

It has been a very rough start to this adventure. I feel maybe Evil has literally done everything it could to hinder any positive outcome. Everything from arguments with Vic, to missed line boats, to the discovery of a very real threat to my children back home. When I talked with Vic this morning, I learned that there has been an outbreak (136 cases) of Dengue Fever, in our neighborhood alone, back in Minas. I have entrusted William, Phillip, and Matthew entirely to His care. Don't know of anything else I can do from here.

Today represents a sort of 'rebirth' for me in many ways. The last six months I spent in the USA, trying to piece my life back together, was difficult. Kansas City was cold and lonely. As I left home to come up here a few days ago, things around me and Vic seemed terminal. Alcohol has come back into the picture again. I can't seem to shake it completely, even after the friends in Texas tried helping me through a treatment center during a serious stooper and a woman or two. Just don't know where to turn. So, I'll just move on, trusting there is Godly rhyme and reason to it all...

Dona Grace and husband, Herbert, put me up at their home last night. They own the "Bem-Bom" Restaurant in Oriximina and probably give away as much food as they sell. I had "Dad's air-conditioned room" to sleep in last night. Air conditioning is rare in these parts. This truly helped me to recover from the two-day boat ride down river from Manaus and all the drinking it entailed. Just don't know what to do with all that's in my heart and mind. I know the drinking isn't the answer. But, *nothing else tends to quiet me as it does*...

Before bedtime, I went down to the dock to meet Gilberto and family for the first time. I set up a meeting with Carlos Augusto of the Medical School here as well. We are to discuss the possibility of an Optometry Partnership between his school and Oklahoma. Dr. M., who came on a trip two years ago, is hoping this can come about. So, do I. It's now 10 P.M. I couldn't bear the thought of staying awake with my *thoughts* – wouldn't have worked well, by myself, in this room. Went out and got a last half-liter of vodka. Should take care of me until I can have more people around. Feeling a little scared of being alone right now.

March 21: I slept well – woke up in sort of a daze. I can't say I feel very well. Alcohol works well while I'm drinking it. Within minutes of waking up to the prospect of not taking a drink, my whole mind, and body seem to shut down. Feels horrible... Since I've returned from the States, I've found out something about myself. The closeness that God allowed me to Himself while alone in the USA, is a feeling that has slowly dwindled upon arriving back home. I guess I could blame it on a number of things, but I won't. The reason is clear. I've allowed my fear of rejection and anxiety around my home life to filter out what God was beginning to teach me through consistent, daily, abiding in Him. I have failed miserably at trying to juggle my fleshly reactions to day-to-day situations and my spiritual survival, much less, growth.

About the only answer I have to this dilemma at this point is, there is no such thing as juggling the things of this world with the things of the spirit. I have become acutely aware of the fact that I must, once and for all, choose the realm in which I will live. I look at the boys, Vic, my work, and my spirit, and find that I will be of absolutely no good to any of them if I opt for anything other than the Spirit's direction and control over my whole being. I so desperately desire the power of the Spirit in my life and realize that it will only come through consistent, persistent "seeking, and I shall find" and "knocking, and it shall be opened to me."

Poor Vic. I have taken that humble, beautiful girl from the farm on a rollercoaster ride of more than 10 years now. She never signed up for the pain I know I've caused her. Don't know how it's possible to have been so pathetic regarding her. There hasn't been a single week of our marriage when she could be certain I would not drink. All I know to do from here is try and control it better. She has become a bitter, suspicious woman during these years. I can't blame her. Can't blame her at all.

God has blessed me beyond my wildest dreams by providing for my family for the coming year. I do not know of many men in this world who have been given such a gift. I have no other option, or desire, in being a good steward of this blessing other than to dedicate my entire time during this period to asking the Holy Spirit to instruct me, fill me with Himself, and protect me from the fiery darts of Evil, as He teaches me.

I do not know where to begin, other than to know that I am forgiven; cast all my anxieties upon Him; and to open myself up fully to His leadership. Even now, at this beginning point, I am filled with anxiety over failure due to unknown trials that might be brought upon by home, children, family, finances, etc. I beg the Holy Spirit give me peace in these areas. Evil is already defeating me before I start, or so it seems. But, I tell you what, God *will* take care of Dengue, the kids, my marriage, my finances, much better than I am able to. All I need do is abide in Him, trust His sovereignty, and know that He has a perfect plan in mind for us all and will work all things out for good.

Oriximina - Trombetas River

The meeting went well with Carlos Augusto this morning. He is a fine young man, very dedicated to his work at the hospital and medical school here in Oriximina. We hacked out the beginnings of a partnership. We shall see from here...

Was underway with Gilberto and family about 1 P.M. No alcohol aboard at all. Not even rubbing alcohol! Their little boat is quite nice. Don't yet know where all five of us are going to sleep for the next couple of nights, but I guess I'll find out soon enough. I've been looking forward to the absence of alcohol during these days. My mind needs to clear. I'm torn up inside right now. It's taking longer and longer to rise from the fog before these trips. I pray God will liberate me from this craziness. I am exhausted...

I felt compelled to ask this simple and dedicated man of God concerning the Holy Spirit. We talked the entire trip to Samauma. It was a challenge, trying to make ourselves heard above the heroic efforts of our small engine. The noise did, however, keep me focused on what was being said, so I missed nothing.

Gilberto spoke of the fact that it was obvious that I truly desired *more* of the Spirit and to experience being filled by Him. Gilberto's opinion, deduced from better than five hours of conversation, is simply this: God desires to give me of Himself and His presence more so than even I want Him to. I must simply not give up asking. I must confess all of my un-confessed wrongs to Him, accept His forgiveness and continually, consistently, and patiently wait on Him. He will reveal Himself as I am ready. So, it's my unconfessed sins that stand in the way...

We had a delicious meal of liver and onions, rice, beans, farinha and bread. I know this family doesn't eat like this when I'm not here, and they wouldn't take any money for supplies prior to this trip. I must figure a way to repay them. We had another couple of hours of conversation, and then we hung our hammocks.

March 22: I awoke at 4:40 this morning to an eerie mixture of howler-monkeys voicing themselves in the distance and Sylvester's relentless snoring right beside me. My mind was filled with thoughts of my boys, Dengue Fever, etc. All I knew to do was to pray for them right then and there. I pray God's protection on them, and the other children threatened at this very moment. I love them even more than I ever imagined is possible. As David put it, *"they are my treasures from God."* I so wish to have them with me throughout my life. I think of the father I have been to them. It is depressing to come to the conclusion I may be no better than a "sperm donor" might have been. I have been absent from them, even when with them. The look in their eyes when they see a beer in my hand is one of almost fear. What a terrible thing to see. Women are not a problem if I am not drinking. I've also never had an affair with one unless I was officially separated from Vic. At least I feel I haven't been unfaithful to her. God help me with all this, please.

We had a leisurely breakfast. My coffee was a bit strong and bitter, but gratefully had no sugar. After the first couple of cups I, as gracefully as possible, poured as much hot water into my thermos as it would hold to dilute the brew. I imagine I could probably make *several* pots with the powder it took to make this single one...

Sunday School got lazily started at about 8:30 A.M. I was introduced and we began. These are very, very simple people. It is a tremendous blessing for me to travel and co-exist with them on a level that I have never before experienced. This is humbling. I feel like 'nobody' next to these people, and I guess I'm really not.

Gilberto had an interesting order-of-service. We sang a bit and then he asked me to read the Scripture passage of my choice. He then preached on that Scripture. Come to find out, by observation, Gilberto reads very little (pretty much only the Bible) and writes even less. So, there are no written sermon notes and he preaches what the Holy Spirit tells him to, at the moment he hears that portion of Scripture. Pretty interesting. However, I would dare to say, it leaves a *whole lot of room* for what might be considered personal views and opinions in the mix of what he says...

After church, we had pirarucu prepared in a couple of different ways. What a treat for me. Then we headed for Lago Batata II. Much more great conversation as we traveled. We arrived at 4 P.M.

We went up to look at the building site. Kentucky's team will be coming here in June. What a breath-taking view of the lake from the top of that hill...

We got things arranged with local leaders to use the school and pavilion for the medical portion of our work. They have a nice, new school that hasn't even been inaugurated yet. As I looked through it, I could almost visualize the blood, teeth, and chaos that will be all over the place in about 90 days. Ah, our groups can reduce most *any* respectable place into havoc and chaos in no time, flat!

We had church again this evening. A storm had set in for the night. Only a handful of folks showed up, but it was a great service, in spite of the storm. Boy, did this building leak! They really need a decent place in which to worship. You know? I often question the amount of money we spend building church buildings all over the place. Seems to me we could all just meet in each other's houses when we need or want to. Those I've seen around here are *more* than ample and have *far* fewer leaks than this place. I don't see how God would be offended by a better use of resources He gives us.

It's really storming right now. We've decided against traveling tonight. Will wait till morning. I don't know what the delay will do to the rest of my trip. I was supposed to be in Obidos in the morning. Oh, well. It will be as it will be.

March 23: We got underway at 5:30 A.M. I slept unusually well and peacefully. A far cry from the last couple of nights. I'm not shaking as much as I was. The alcohol seems to be out of my system. I thank God for that. We should be in Oriximina by 11 this morning. I believe I can catch the bus to Obidos at 1:30 P.M. I look forward to calling Vic and the boys as soon as I can get to a phone. It will be great just to confirm God's wonderful watch-care over my children and their mother.

I'm sitting out here on the "duck bill" of our tiny boat, enjoying the cruise. I can imagine having my boys with me out here at some point in the future. This is truly a life and place I desire to share and maybe pass on to them. We have so very much of this world that is insignificant and unneeded. There is a vast bank of wonder and knowledge that we can learn through the complex simplicity of God's creation. It is impossible and even ludicrous to try and measure it by society's educational, cultural, and financial standards. These "standards" just don't apply here. I often question their validity at all…

I've had sweet, rambling talks with Gilberto all morning. We've talked about everything from the history of this area, to hunting techniques and philosophies, to the great loss that we've both experienced with the death of good friends. It's been a good morning. I almost wish I could end the trip right here. I really don't want to switch gears to my next stop and host in Obidos. But, I know it will be something I wouldn't want to miss.

Missed the bus to Obidos so, I hired a Jon-boat to take me just as soon as we arrived in Oriximina. I felt it is important to stay on the move. If I were to have to spend a night alone, I would certainly drink. Trying to avoid that. It's been several days since my last debacle. Don't want to risk staring it all over again. The extra expense for the boat ride was certainly worth it.

Before I left, I was able to get in touch with both Vic and Dad. Praise God, the boys are indeed o.k.! Vic is not nearly as concerned now, as she was a couple days ago. She spoke to a doctor friend who lives in our apartment building. He's managed to calm her down. I prefer to acknowledge God's answer to *my* prayers. Poor Phillip answered the phone when I called. I, naturally, asked how he was feeling. I asked him if he had Dengue. He said, "Yeah, everybody does!" I just about died!! I rudely told him to let me talk to the maid or *somebody* that could answer my questions! All ended well. I trust he'll forgive me for my rudeness.

The trip to Obidos took about 50 minutes. That little boat about beat me to death! But really, I had no choice. When I arrived, Pastor Alberto was already waiting as planned. I got a bite to eat at a local "greasy spoon" café and we were off again by 3 P.M. This promises to be a very different experience for me than that of the past few days.

We arrived in Mamauru at 3:50 P.M. What a great homecoming! It was so good to see so many familiar faces -- most of which have no names to me anymore, but they are friends, none the less. The names will be coming back to me, one at a time.

It was great to see Buko again – the "gentle giant." I've often thought of him over the years. I'll always remember that when he was asked what he planned for himself in the 'future', he sat pensively for a good while, and then answered with a profound question of his own, "You mean tomorrow?" If only I could see it all that way...

I invited Buko to come along for the ride to Flexal, spend a couple of days with me. The Arkansas team will be working there the first part of July. Pastor Paulo asked for a ride as well, along with his 8-year-old. I have one of those at home, too. Of course, I said yes...

Alberto's boat is quite large. Compared to Gilberto's, this one could comfortably sleep 25! On our way, we stopped and bought a fresh, surubim catfish for dinner. Buko let me prepare it under his watchful eye, of course. I must admit, I made a fantastic fish stew with rice, all the way from cleaning the fish, to serving the final product. How good it was! We arrived at our destination at 8 P.M.

I've rarely traveled in this way. How refreshing to actually *not* be in charge, *not* to have an agenda other than planning and seeing old friends, able to stop and visit *at will* on the level of the people and not as some task-oriented, far-off, detached, shell of a person that can neither touch nor be touched. What a relief. How incredibly refreshing. I could have actually brought some alcohol along on this trip. Alberto and Buko know I have a glass from time to time. Glad I didn't though. Need to be without for a while.

Alberto, Buko and I had some good talks. The nature of *these* conversations has been much lighter than those with Gilberto. Paulo went to his home as soon as we arrived. We then backed off and cast anchor for the night.

March 24: I slept much better last night, and was up at the usual 5:30 A.M. Not shaking at all. At least not on the outside. I know from experience the "inner- tremors" will take a little while longer to subside. We took our time fixing breakfast – eggs, bread, coffee. We three had a good time of sharing. We, of course, talked about the Holy Spirit – contrasting fruits of the flesh with fruits of the Spirit using Paul's letter to the Galatians. We touched a bit on alcohol and other things considered as "fruits of the flesh". Once again, the 'sin' thing came up. I wish I could fully see it that way. Not sure why I can't. There seems to be something far deeper and far-reaching that requires a definition of something more than just a 'sin'. Or, maybe I'm just trying to be special within my particular struggles. Lord, help me...

The church in Mamauru is dead due to in-fighting, dissension , factions – things I believe to be common to most all, local churches.

In my view, this phenomenon is due to the 'human factor'. Much healing must take place. In this particular case, I believe it the fault of the American group who began this good work several years ago, but has since abandoned it, not even to lift it up in prayer. What a terrible sin against God and this precious people. I wonder if these "zealot Christians" who come storming down here, proclaiming the Good News once in a blue moon, would starve their own children after giving birth to them? I think not.

After some contemplation, I think this little church may serve God best by disbanding and starting over with as little outside influence as possible, concentrating of the only thing that is important – studying Scripture and, as God gives them understanding, pass on what they learn by sharing *only Christ* with those who have need of Him. *Forget* all the bullshit dogma and denominationalism that confuses and causes strife among them!

Well, Paulo's father-in-law is dying here in Flexal. We paid him a visit. He's really in bad shape with a lung infection of some kind. There's already a death rattle. I've heard it a hundred times. So, the end is imminent. He was a true blessing to me. Here is a man that is dying, yet totally at peace, and smiling at the prospect. The odd thing here is that all around him are people praying for a miracle of healing. I believe he and I were the only ones silently asking God to take him home – soon. He's 79 years old. I'll never make it that far. I think he and I both, are ready to go.

We left Flexal at 10 A.M. after buying some more fish – One surubim catfish weighing 6 kg and Six Tucunare bass at a total of 6 kg. We left four of the bass with Paulo's wife and kept two for ourselves. The surubim will find its designated owner somewhere, later today.

Guess what? I fixed the bass up in stew, all by myself. It was great! Buko still looked on closely, beings he was going to have to eat it... I had all the time in the world to fix lunch because Alberto has, once again, managed to get us *completely* gift-wrapped in floating grass! I swear the man can't come within 100 meters of the stuff without getting us hopelessly stuck in the middle of it...

Castanhanduba

We stopped off in Castanhanduba at 3 P.M. to say "hello" to Lindomar, the church, and his boat, the "*Roy-Ruby*". This little vessel was purchased by two brothers from Arkansas back in 1987 and has been plowing the waters of these lakes and rivers ever since. Lindomar wasn't here, but everything seems in good shape. We bought what was left of today's bread, made by Lindomar, and a spoonful of butter for a snack. We helped build the little bakery, years ago, to help support he and his family. Sure, glad we did it. The fruit of *that* effort will be eaten today!

I had a lengthy talk with Buko as we cruised. He's been away from the church for about six months now – just got tired of all the usual things that people tend to get tired of in their local churches. He was accused of 'hidden cigarette smoking' and just decided it was time to go. I can't really blame him. Just one of the '150,000 *self-righteous rules*' thrown in by the asshole, missionaries who brought the Gospel to this area, decades ago. It is also why I have as little to do with them as possible, still today. It seems I spend more time 'un-teaching' the useless junk our poor people have been taught, than I do sharing the truth of the Gospel...

By the end of our conversation, which included a couple of cigarettes between us, I feel that he will put it all behind him and return to the church. He would make such a fine leader, but God, not I, will have to show him. He has such a sweet spirit. People, especially the young, would naturally follow him. We'll see how it goes...

After dropping Bauldo off and getting underway, I truly don't know how, *or when*, I'm going to make it home! I'm about 4 hours from Obidos right now. The last bus to Oriximina left two hours ago. It seems kind of strange, yet totally unalarming, that I am supposed to be on a plane out of Trombetas in about 14 hours, but there just doesn't seem to be any way to get there by then. Oh, well, we shall see.

We arrived in Obidos at 5:30 P.M. I walked some 35 km (more like 100 meters), with all my bags, to Alberto's house! I took a good, ice cold bath, re-scheduled my flight to leave from Santarem and had some eggs and bread. All should be well till morning. Had a good visit with the "Alberto family." His kids have all grown like weeds since I last saw them several years ago...

I left at 7:30 P.M. to try to find a boat for Santarem. Guess what? I'm taking the "*Nadison*", again! Walmike was on hand to make certain that I got my usual, owners' suite. Such a blessing. I should arrive in Santarem at about three in the morning and on to be at the airport by 6:00. I guess I won't see my brother's kids this time around. I would like to, but the schedule doesn't seem to be working out that way

One of the better "Line-boats"

We got underway at 8:40 P.M. It was great talking to Dad before I left Obidos. All is well there. From now own, when he comes this way to travel on one of our pastor's boats, I'll be able to visualize what he's experiencing. What a simple, no frills time this has been. To most people we describe this "life-style" to, it all seems *far* too primitive to endure. But those of us who have experienced it, love it, and look forward to the 'next time, with fond memories to keep us going. What an adventure. The pace is slow; we bathe in the river; the food is simple; the fellowship is unmatched, anywhere; the blessings are too many to recount. This is surely what God had in mind for his creation from the very start. We've kinda fouled that up though...

March 25: It is odd how quickly things can change for me. How soon I can determine an 'about-face' along an otherwise, steady course. We docked at the Santarem port sometime during the night. I woke up at 5:20 A.M., sharp. It is now 6:06 A.M. and I'm here at the airport. Just finished 'bribing' the night watchman to unlock the cooler at the bar and let me pay him for some beers.

My soul is cleaving to the dust right now. I feel truly lost and empty, even after all the amazing things God has allowed me to see and learn in these past days. I have no idea what to do with myself. This trip is practically over. I am on my way back to a home more broken than I left it, with a heart more broken than ever before. Here we go again. God, help me. Help me, please...

> *Alcohol is, indeed, cunning and baffling. In just the few short days, I had gone through the entire cycle of remorse over past actions, identification of the cause, resolve to do better and then, a complete about-face, at the first opportunity I am left to myself. Vic lived with these ever-repeating cycles throughout our 19-year marriage. Never knowing when I might 'fall off the wagon' again. As for me, at this stage in the game, I was seeking only for a way to control my drinking. I had no intention of obtaining completely. The Organization was still relatively safe for I am able to 'manage' it in virtual seclusion from the world. I could still make rational decisions regarding the path forward and what was best for our teams and the communities where they worked.*
>
> *Things are about to get much worse. As of the end of this journal, I had no idea just how far my resolve, morals and subsequent behavior would decline – Just how damaging alcohol would become, as its power over me subtly increased...*

CHAPTER TWO

From 'building' to 'destroying' in just 12 days...

On the eve of this trip, it seemed my marriage was over, yet salvageable – quite a contradiction of terms. Vic and I had agreed to try for a healthy relationship, just one last time. We both had our doubts but were willing to continue for the benefit of the boys. If there was any love left at all, we would need to discover it together.
I had taken on a new President back in 1996 to help us continue our growth in the USA while I concentrated more on the field in the Amazon. After a three-year trial, I'd found that the leadership I'd put in place had been divisive and corrupt. They had misappropriated funds and struck 'agreements' with politicians and businesses which amounted to nothing less than racketeering and collusion. One of the purposes of this "fix it trip" is to survey the damage and pick up what pieces that still remained of our hospital and several other assets. My drinking had quelled, but was still playing a very present, dominant role in everything.

"FIX IT TRIP"
December 05 – 17, 1999

12/05/99

I managed not to drink very much at all while I was home these past couple of weeks. Vic brought me to the airport this morning to catch my flight. Neither of us got much sleep last night with William's party and all. I *did* drink too much, then. Really don't remember much about it. I'm sure when the opportunity is right, Vic will hammer me about it...

Richard called at 3 AM – I was dead asleep. Vic answered the phone. He has misplaced his passport. Well, if he is there in Manaus on Tuesday, he's there. If not, he's not. I truly looked forward to the week we would spend together. It is in God's hands – just where it should be. No telling what he and Vic talked about, other than his Passport. I know I'll probably be hearing about *that* someday, too.

Vic and I came talking all the way to Belo. We both desire to fall in love with each other again. Just don't know how to go about it or even if it is possible. We talked about it all – the boys, us, past others, etc. She brought up a fact that I had never really considered. In all fairness to her, if we try and fail again over, say, the next 10 years, I will still be ok. For me, at 50 years of age, finding a nice young 20-somethng, will be no problem at all. However, for *her*, by then at age 43, the options would be very limited – I totally agree. It would be very selfish of me to insist on her love for a time, while she runs out of time to have a loving relationship with someone she actually does desire to love – Tough thought for me, but so very true. The fact that I still drink from time to time came up as well. To her, it makes me particularly unpredictable and undependable in her sight. I said that I work hard and provide well. That should count for something. In the end, I guess it doesn't though. I'm a mess...

The other issue, just as important, if not more so, is the boys. We both love them desperately. We both share concern for their feelings, future and proximity to each of us. We are both loving and devoted parents to the little ones God has given to us. We both fear for their emotional and spiritual development and health. We both desire to have them by our side. We both do all that we are able to ensure that they each understand our immense love for them. God can fix all of this. As for me personally, I feel helpless and recognize I have no control over any of this anymore, if I ever did at all. May God give Vic and I the grace to carry on according to His will and not our own... I am really torn right now. I believe that, for the first time, I can accept Vic's need for someone she can love, honor and cherish. Oddly, I do not feel the jealousy that I once did regarding her giving herself to someone else. You know, I must confess that I oscillate on this emotion from day-to-day. But, right now, I wish for her the very feelings that I wish to have for someone – I miss the intimacy and fellowship. If I desire this for myself, why should I deny the same for her?

I tell you what, I have much to take care of on this trip. All of this other is preeminent on my mind. I look forward to what God is going to do over the next couple of weeks. I feel that He will speak to me, very specifically, regarding many issues in my life.

My flight's been delayed. Having a few beers while I wait. Feels good to be somewhat free of the "Homefront" for a while. However good the conversation was on the way over here, I need some relief from it all. So much stress.

12/06/99

Arrived in Manaus and got settled in the hotel about 9 last night. I drank so much on the plane and during the lay-over in Brasilia, I can't remember even falling asleep. Got up this morning and had a couple of beers to get going. Feeling pretty rough.

Ended up being a productive day. Looked at the generator for the *Belatis*. Seems the price went from R$10,500.00 to R$7,900.00 – I can't believe it! Thank God.

Went and bought a speedboat for our work. It's great. 21' x 5'. Has all the needed things, e.g. steering, controls, dry well, dry-storage, etc. I will feel more comfortable now with Dad using it by himself. I'll name it the "*WilPhilMatt*", after my boys.

The WilPhilMatt

Talked to Vic a couple of times this morning. Thank God all is well at home and she didn't seem to know I'd had a couple of beers. Cell phones are a threat to me sometimes. She can call me anytime. If I don't answer, she assumes I've been drinking. If I answer, she *knows* I've been drinking. What a deal... My plans are to catch a line-boat tomorrow afternoon for Oriximina so that I can accompany the *WilPhilMatt*. Still have a lot to do today. It's raining like crazy here in Manaus. So, what else is new!?!

I am really going to miss Richard's company on this adventure. I just wish that God had had other plans. I need time with Richard. He always seems to shed light on questions I have regarding my life. Richard is one of four men that God has placed on this earth, I feel, on my behalf. The other three being Dad, Donald and Albert. These guys' have always been at the right place, at the right time for me. I have never been able to reciprocate in any way for the blessing they have been to me over the years. Maybe someday, somehow.

The day ended well. Had dinner at a "greasy spoon" down the street. Good food – I'll probably pay for it tomorrow, though. Got calls from Dona Grace and Carlos Augusto this afternoon. They are anxiously awaiting my arrival – must have some issues to discuss. This trip is all about "issues". May God give me wisdom, patience and discernment.

12/07/99
Long tough day. Felt dazed all morning. Finally, Wellington bought a little cooler to carry in the back seat with me. If I hadn't been able to have a beer every now and then, I don't think I could have made it. The feeling I get after drinking a little too much the night before is horrible. I strangely feel I could die at any moment. My hands shake and sweat, and I feel like throwing up but can't. Need to get this under control. I waste a lot of time in the mornings like this. Tonight, I'll just have a couple, if any, and lay down.

Getting the proper documentation for the *WilPlilMatt* was "trying" to say the least. Believe it or not, I had to go through two sets of 'false documents' before the store owner finally gave me the real ones that would be required to cross the Para State border. What these guys will do to try and get out of paying the taxes they don't want to pay...

I'm aboard the *Nadison Jeanne IV*, in a cabin. These people are great. When they saw me coming, they brought me straight here, to the owner's suite, at the price of a regular cabin. The refrigerator, of course, is full... I missed speaking to Vic before I traveled. My cell signal was too weak at the port. I tried and tried but kept getting a busy signals on my end. I'd like to have a beer now that we are getting underway. Maybe it's just as well.

The cabin is cool and clean. I haven't been on this boat in a long time. It is the one we rented for the Crandall group to build the "Linda Amor" Clinic about 7 years ago. Kind of ironic that I am on-board again headed, ultimately, to determine the fate of that very Clinic. I depend on you Lord. I am Yours to be used as you see fit.

When I get off by myself like this, I really come in contact with the reality of my need of the Lord, every step of the way. In solitude, my dependence on Him becomes overwhelming. You know, when I am home with Vic and the boys, there is a sense of solidarity and belonging as I plan for trips such as this. I feel secure and confident – less dependent on the Lord. More dependent on logic. Now I am here with so very much to take care of and accomplish. I feel unworthy. I just try and rest in the Lord. Knowing that He is in control now, not I.

My brother called this morning from the USA. With Richard not coming, the "Christmas Box" for his children won't make it either. He asked me to buy some gifts to take to them. I know exactly how he feels right now. I missed Christmas and birthdays with my precious ones last year – it was tough.

I flew my brother back to the US about a year ago. He was suffering from a deep depression of some kind and need treatment. We hired a phycologist for him and he's on some medication to help lift his spirits. He was drinking too much and self-medicating a bit. Just caught up with him I guess. It's been a wakeup call for me. Need to control my stuff or I might have a problem myself, someday.

12/08/99
It is 5 AM. The accommodations are great here on the *Nadison*. However, I didn't sleep restfully last night. Spent most of it emptying the fridge and avoiding outside and the company it sometimes brings. Don't need any of *that* to further complicate matters. I woke up on the floor, wadded up in a sheet. Have no idea how that happened.

They brought me dinner last night – insisted that I eat in peace away from the crowd. The fact that we've spent around 30K renting their vessels over the years, I believe, doesn't really matter anymore. I think they just appreciate what we represents to the Valley. It's humbling to feel welcomed everywhere I go on this mighty river. It is a respect that I never asked or planned for. It just happened gradually over the years though actions directed by God.

I've been thinking about the trip this morning. How I should make it. I would love to just grab Cako in Oriximina, fuel-up the WilPhilMatt and take off. Too bad Cako will be out with the Mayor on the *Belatis*. We've loaned it to him for a 10-day trip. Oh well, those are the breaks I guess. Line-boats, it will be...

Been thinking much about Vic and me. She will be moving to Vitoria, Espirito Santo during the first quarter of 2000. Vic has secured a position with her old company to help with a 3-4-year project they have just won the bid on over there. She will be "Project Coordinator" in Vitoria. The pay isn't a big issue here, but for her career, it's a MAJOR plus. It will be good for me also. Only 15 minutes to the airport instead of 3-4 hours. My main desire is that we are *together* in this move. I will go wherever my children are – I just desire that it be as a family. I don't want to make a move like last time. Don't want to rent a house across the street from them. We may also be able to enroll the boys in an English-speaking school. Their academic future needs to be in English.

The move will be a plus for us. We can get away from family and "friends". Maybe grow to depend on each other again. Also, Simolton, has a church there. He is anointed as Richard is. This association would be healthy for us. Maybe just another affirmation for the move.

I was able to sleep a part of the day today. Our arrival time in Oriximina is confirmed for 7PM. I should get there just in time to get a good night's sleep! I'm looking forward to the days ahead. So very much might be accomplished.

12/09/99
Arrived in Oriximina on time last night. Don't remember sleeping much. It was hot – no breeze. At least I didn't feel any mosquitoes. The beers I bought at the port would have kept me numb even if there *were* mosquitoes.

Upper Deck of the Belatis

Got up early this morning. It is good to be aboard the *Belatis* once again, if only for a day or two before she sails.

She's been a home and refuge for 10 years now. Seen bits and pieces of me the world best not be aware of.

Spent the entire day getting the motor and controls adapted to the *WilPhilMatt*. Had lunch at the "Bem Bom" – good visit with Grace and Bauldo even though it was a struggle eating just a spoonful of food. My goodness. Seems I either eat or I drink. Can't seem to do both...

Also visited with Pr. Pedro. We will leave in the morning to visit the church and Institute in Carimum. Jonas, Pr. Pedro's father, will be going with us to get an estimate on materials needed to complete the Institute building. This little trip should be a good test-run for the *WilPhilMatt*.

I can't believe this – it's after 10 PM and the mechanic *just now* finished all the adaptations on the *WilPhilMatt*. So much for "just drop the motor on and go"... All in all, a pretty productive day. Scheduled to leave for Carimum at 6 in the morning. I'm looking forward to it very much. But, for now, I just want to relax a little and get some sleep...

12/10/99

Early start today. Up at 5 AM – got the boat fueled and we was headed up the Trombetas River by just after 6. What a trip! Thoroughly enjoyed the fellowship with Pr. Pedro and his father. The WilPhilMatt performed like a top. Very fast, smooth and stable. We made Oriximina to Carimum in just 45 minutes. Did the estimate on materials to finish-out the Institute. Looks like we are basically going to have to start from scratch. It seems that the original "builders" were a bit haphazard in their ways. There are roofs where they should not be – walls where none are needed – and floors in areas where no one will walk or stand. Oh well, their intentions were good anyway, I guess.

Went a little further up the lake and visited Tiburcio and his family. They have a mentally challenged son. It took the entire visit, and all the chewing gum I had in my pocket, for him to warm-up to me. All is well with the church there. The river has already started rising. However, it is still very, very low. The fishing must be fantastic about now...

It is noon and I'm back here on the *Belatis*. Herbert just left. We went over all the changes and repairs to be made on her over the next few months. It is a lot of work. The kitchen will be re-done, adding a door to the flap at the stern. The cabin upstairs will be increased in size by almost double. The upper decks will be redone, and a new roof will be put on. She will be pulled, re-caulked and painted. A new generator and wiring will be installed. Each item is costly, but very much needed for the years of trips to come. Hope the funds hold-up...

Carlos Augusto and Dona Mira will be on-board to discuss our "possible" partnership. Alberto should be here shortly after that. I hope he is. It would save me a trip to Obidos.

I feel terrible right now. Haven't been able to calm my nerves at all today. Wish I didn't have to at all. The trip up to Carimum was a good distraction but now I'm alone and feeling shaky. Can hardly wait for all the meeting to end.

Carlos and Mira from the Universidade Federal Fluminense showed up right on time. I was totally up-front with them regarding the status of our project. The status is, simply, that there is no status – We are still working toward a spring of 2000 date. I left everything set with them on this end. It is now up to the US university to get off their royal asses and take care of business. We have to get a "trial-run" under our belts to get things started.

Conseicao, Alberto's wife, just came in from Obidos with a group from their church. There is a big 'revival' beginning tonight. Anyway, she told me Alberto is waiting for me in Obidos. Here I am, waiting for him here in Oriximina... Oh well, I'll catch the 9PM boat to Obidos. He will pick me up at the port there sometime after 11 tonight. It's 2 PM right now. I have time for a few final beers and a nap before I see him. Thank God. At least I'll feel a little better by then.

I had a very troubling phone conversation with Vic this afternoon. I just pray God will give each of us the grace to trust each other. We say and think things that a most definitely untrue about each other. Separation is gaining ground – Oh God, handle this, please. I'm about out of energy to handle it myself. Her figuring out I'd had a few beers didn't help matters either. If she only knew how much her accusatory attitude has to do with it. Maybe she would tone things down if she did.

Arrived on schedule here in Obidos. Had pizza with Alberto at his house. He's going to take the rest of this trip with me. What a blessing. It won't be like having Richard with me, but Alberto is definitely a true man of God. I look forward to the fellowship with him over the next 5-6 days. It will be good for our Spirits. It is now 1 AM – I am exhausted – I need to get some rest.

12/11/99
Short night – up at 6 AM. Feeling like crap this morning. Woke-up determined to speak with Vic anyway. She called at a little past 9 AM. All she says she wants is the truth when she asks me something. My conscious is clear that I have already done this. You know, I've always been afraid to "tell all" to her for fear that she would misunderstand me. She claims the opposite to be true. It just seems that I am always on the defensive regarding things that are complete fabrications of her mind. The people, places and things are true enough – the context and content of those people, places and things, are in her mind. I really don't know what to do about this

ridiculous situation. It is not right that I should have to continually walk on eggshells. Am I to confess to stuff I haven't done, so she can feel better about herself? I think not.

Alberto and I am aboard the *Jeanne-Carlos* right now, waiting to depart for Santarem. We just got here after having lunch at Edison's house. They had a split in the church here a couple of month's back. Things are just getting back to normal. The whole issue was over the "reform" movement ("Pentcostalizing" things). Unfortunately, Abiezer was involved in it all...

The pastor and I had a great visit along the way. We discussed all of the little "problems" with the various works, Paranorte, the hospital, etc. Neither of us have any problems with the individuals involved, only disappointments... Lucifer and Levando have played a very underhanded game with people and assets. They have lied to and manipulated individuals, organizations and churches, both in the USA and here. It is just a matter of time before they are exposed and irradiated. I pray God's mercy upon them when this actually occurs. Actually, God forgive me, I look forward to the crash. I, as much as anyone, know the cost that must be paid for actions. A price *must* be paid for wrong action. But, as no other, I know that the grace of God is faithful to comfort, restore and fortify – we need but to ask, in sincerity, humility and profound dependence. I trust these guys realize this when they get hit and fall on their asses.

I took 3 alprazolam and actually got a couple hour nap on the way to Santarem. Feel reasonably well. So glad I wrote myself a script before leaving home. I'd be in a bad situation if I hadn't.

Well, it's just after 6 PM. We arrived here in Santarem just in time to transfer to our next boat, the *Leao III*, thirty minutes ago, headed to Aveiro. The whistle is blowing right now as we pull away.

Aboard the Leao III

This is *unreal!*

No cabins available for our stuff. So, I've got my stuff; my brother's kid's Christmas stuff and Alberto's stuff, all crammed under my hammock. I'll be lucky if I don't end up impregnated by a "suitcase" before we arrive.

We are packed in here, (on the bottom floor) 3-deep. It will be a miracle if all our baggage, and we, make it to Aveiro in one piece! I am laying here in my hammock writing this, without being able to move my elbows at all – I just shift the legal pad into position under my pen as I write. Just like an old typewriter... Gonna be *some* night, huh Lord!? I'm *definitely* not complaining about it – I need to travel this way from time to time to truly appreciate what God has blessed me with in the *Belatis*... Thanks' to the "diazepam gods" I think we'll make it through the night...

12/12/99
Believe it or not, I got a little sleep along the way. Arrived in Aveiro at 5:30 this morning – still have my "sea legs", wobbling around like the drunk that I am... The hospital looks beautiful – very clean and well kept. Funny how God works things out. We came completely

unannounced to try and figure out who we needed to talk to about resolving the issues involving our hospital. I already knew that the major hang-ups were the signatures of the Mayor and the Secretary of Health on a document requesting association with the National Health Department (SUS). The Mayor simply does not wish to sign such an agreement on behalf of the local Community Association. He wants the contract to be with him so that he can control the funds that will come in (all the more money for him to pilfer from).

When we arrived, we went straight to Wilson's house (he is our Chaplain at the clinic). Woke everybody up. Just so happens that there is a meeting of the Community Association and the Community Health Council scheduled for 9:30 this morning. This meeting is also to include the Mayor and Health Secretary. The discernment God *will* give me during this meeting will also give the decision that I must make regarding the future of this clinic.

I am emotionally touched by all of this. I am walking though the clinic right now. There are photographs of my father, holding little children, on the walls. Many of me, too. Boy, I was young back then… This place was built and dedicated to help others in Jesus' Name. It should remain that way. If only the politics would "disappear". Evidently, Levando Veloso and Lucifer Haggard have really screwed things up. I do not know what they were trying to accomplish in their negotiations, other than financial gain for themselves. That fact is obvious through what everyone has told me and the documentation that has been presented me here. Whatever it was, it jeopardized everything for the past year or better. What evil men…

It is now 5:05 PM. We are aboard the *Madeirinha*, headed back to Santarem. What a day. God is unbelievable in His ways. The 9:30 meeting began "promptly" at 10:15. The Council insisted that I sit at the head of the table. I just wanted to listen but became more and more involved as the meeting developed. Just so happens that *both* the Mayor and Health Secretary were absent. They had "suddenly" traveled last night (yeah, really..). There were, however, 4 County Commissioners present (enough for a legislative quorum). One of the Commissioners happened to be the Chairperson of the Board of Commissioners. Much recently disclosed corruption, on the part of the Mayor, Health Secretary, Veloso and Hagar was brought to light for the first time. The Commissioners and Council Members became indignant. Come to find out, some US$ 13,000.00 per month had been received this year by the Mayor, designated for "municipal health". Not one dime had been passed on to the health facilities here. As a matter of fact, he had fired all of the nurses and nurses' aides, saying that there was simply no money coming in for health. What a thieving, lying ass!!

The result: Well, the Chair of the City Council is the "acting Mayor and Health Secretary" in official meetings. She, therefore, proceeded to sign, on their behalf of the absent parties, the document that had been tabled for over a year. The deal was done.

I later met with the Community Association that has been and will continue to run the clinic. I told them that our funding to them would now end. They asked that, if possible, these funds could continue until the end of April, until they could get on their feet. I said yes. The request to me for survival funds for them to continue to work, humbled me deeply – reminded me like a slap in the face of what God was providing me and my family through His kindness. Because of this, I can do what God has called me to do. I also told Wilson that his support would continue until he relocated, if he indeed does. I was made a "Lifetime" member of the Administrative Council of the Association – strictly honorary, I'm sure. This should really make Lucifer's bunch *very* happy campers... In a day, the business it took them better than a year to screw-up, was resolved. Makes me wonder a bit about actions and results of the "flesh".

They just haven't worked at taking care of God's business – Lord, let me never 'live' there again... The reason is now clear why they didn't want to retain the Clinic. It would now cost them money, yielding no return, because their ability to stealing has now ceased. On the other hand, the boats they have stolen from us will yield them contributions, from unsuspecting people back in the USA, for years to come. Oh well, at least they are "calculating" thieves. Oh, I just heard that Lucifer's investment business back home has just had its license suspended due to 'questionable practices'. And, the dominoes begin to fall...

All in all, a marvelous 12 hours in Aveiro. The clinic will survive and thrive, and I will be out from under obligations to it within a few months. Only, I repeat, *Only* the power of the Holy Spirit of God could have accomplished what was accomplished this day.

12/13/99
Arrived in Santarem at 4:30 this morning. We caught a cab to my brother's house to deliver the presents to the kids. Woke everybody up. These precious children really miss their father... I had to go out back a couple of times to cry a bit – It was overwhelming to hear their questions and not have a clear answer for them as to when their daddy would be home again. There is something terribly wrong with all of this. I know, because I have been through it before, more than once, myself. I pray God never permits me to be separated, indefinitely, from my family again – It is debilitating and devastating, to say the very least. The will to live vanishes quickly. There is no amount of "conforming" or "adjusting" that could possibly make such things to feel "ok".

Was at the airport with Alberto by 6:00 AM – All flights to Parintins were sold-out for the day. So, went back to my brother's house. Then, downtown to try and find Levando and Ferriera.

I wanted to ask Levando about the most resent boat he took from Alberto. There was no answer at the door of his house or his phone. I needed to get documents for the Patrice underway with Ferriera (the dispatcher). He wasn't available either. Oh well, struck-out both times. Went from there to the port to reserve space on the next boat to Parintins. We leave early this afternoon on the *Nadison Jeanne IV*. Started trying to get my tickets changed for home for the 17th instead of the 20th. Hope it works out. I feel I real need to get home...

We finally caught a boat. It is scheduled to arrive in Parintins in the morning at 11:00. The connecting boat for Barreirinha leaves Parintins at Noon. Always a close connection, it seems. I am enjoying the "chaos" of the trip. These days with Alberto constantly at my side, have been wonderful; enriching. I look forward to the remaining few that we have left together.

We have been on a total of 5 line-boats. So far, one has been "comfortable" and 4 have been "tolerable, at best". At any rate, it has all been a highly productive experience.

Just had another conversation with Vic. I was feeling so down, having seen my nephews. Just wanted to hear her voice and the fact that my boys are well. Once again, my sweet mother-in-law has taken it upon herself to discuss (out of context and *way* different from our actual visit) a conversation I had with her before departing on this trip. She has jumped all over Vic about "us". This really pisses me off. She has, once again, made Vic out to be the "bad guy" in this whole story. I just want everybody to *shut up* and leave us the hell alone! Vic is going to have to trust me in what I say, and, I, in what she says. I am so angry right now. God's got to do this job – I *know* I've been a screw-up; Vic's done her share, too. We're both at fault here...

I've had time to talk, pray and ponder for a while now. My Lord and God, it is truly in your hands. I recognize the convictions

You've placed in my heart regarding my personal life. Funny thing is, they make the lies that Vic insists on believing, all the more ridiculous in my sight. I truly have *nothing* more to confess, defend or explain to her. I know in my heart that I have held nothing back. If she continues to insist along the lines she is following, *she* will be the miserable one, not I. Evil keeps whispering in her ear. Only God can silence that. Wow, affairs with S and R? At the same time!? How much farther off-base could you get? Vic needs to be careful of the "voices" whispering in her ear...

It is now 5:20 PM. Alberto and I have a cabin for this trip. It is going to be a long one (about 20 hrs.). Should be restful in the a/c. Boat #6 now – this brings the count to 2 "comfortable" ones/4 "tolerable, at best". Odds are getting better! I have been eating whatever they serve on these boats for meals. I must say, they have figured out a way to hide *any* and *everything* you can imagine inside a big pot of soup! Don't get me wrong, it is all pretty tasty. It's just that the ingredients are totally unrecognizable. However, on

the boat last night, I definitely recognized chunks of cow intestines (I *hope* it was from a cow...). At least they cleaned 'em pretty good before dumping them in the stew. Went down pretty well... I'm getting hungry just writing about it – hope the soups' good tonight.

12/14/99

Got to sleep at 9 last night. Had a great study with Alberto on spiritual warfare. We were able to identify several sources of problems in our personal and work lives, as being purely spiritual in nature. It is so important that we be able to recognize the nature of a specific problem. If it is of the flesh, we can usually fix it ourselves. If it is beyond our control or actions, we must look to the spiritual weapons we have at our disposal. We both went to sleep with a renewed determination to discern between the spirits as they enter our minds and the minds with which we come in contact. It is so very important to recognize when forces beyond our control are at work – It is devastating when we don't. I just have a problem with it all. My drinking seems to be something I could and should control. However, when push comes to shove, I feel pushed and shoved beyond my control. Regarding women, I don't ever think about them except during separations with Vic and I am drinking. I pray about this, daily. I am told it all revolves around "sin" having a firm grip on my life. How can this be true if I pray for protection and re-birth, daily? Am I just that weak and ridiculous!? God help me. I'm freakin' confused about my ignorance regarding these specific things...

Took 4 alprazolam before laying down, but as awakened abruptly at 11:00 PM by being thrown from my bed! With the hazed mind of sleep, I got up. The engine had fallen to an idle. I opened the cabin door, fully expecting to see the boat sinking from the impact. In a flash, I thought about going after some "Jonah" to throw overboard. Then, in another flash, I thought that the "Jonah" I sought after, might just be me! Well, end of flashes.... What had happened was, we had run aground, but got off quickly. The rest of the night was restful.

Slept till 5:30. Awakened by the chaos as we pulled into Porto Juruti for a passenger pick-up.

Had breakfast (my usual pot of black coffee), took a shower and shaved. ETA/Parintins is still 11:00 AM. Surely hope so. Our next vessel is supposed to depart for Barreirinha at Noon.

Just talked to the Captain. Our newest ETA is now Noon. This kind of cramps our departure for Barreirinha. We will radio ahead and try to hold the boat till we get there. Just have to see what happens, huh? No need to get anxious. If I did, it would just make me the *only* anxious person in the Amazon Valley. I don't think I want to be in that extreme minority – I'd kinda stick-out in the crowd...

Arrived in Parintins 15 minutes ago. The "Tocantins" (our "canoe" to Barreirinha) should leave at 1:00 PM. It is now 12:45 – Thank God she was running late. Alberto and I are already in our hammocks, claiming our domain. This is a tiny boat. I think we are in for a Looong trip to Barreirinha.

I just realized I haven't had any alcohol for two or three days now. Not shaking anymore, inside *or* out. What a relief. I think I could just do without it for good. Scary thought but I think I could do it if I try.

Just found out our ETA is 5:00 PM – good goal anyway. I'm anxious to get to talk to Pr. Oseas tonight. I really want to know what his needs are; his desires for the work; his concerns. The work has grown so very little over the past 4-5 years. I wonder what he attributes this to. Alberto and I have prayed for wisdom along these very lines. I know we also have the prayers of Dad and Richard right now – This is a reassuring fact for our visits today and tomorrow.

Arrived Barreirinha at 6:00 this evening. The pastor is out visiting (good sign, I guess...). We had a good talk with Dona Cilene. Never know how much of what she says is from her own mind and how much is from the church, in general. But, she can sure talk a guy silly! I've ordered a Tambaqui fish stew for tonight at the restaurant next door to the "Barreirinha Hilton", where we will spend the night. We left a message for Oseas and his wife to meet us at 8:00 for dinner. Well, it's about 7:50 right now. So, better get going. I'm starving!!

Had a *great* meal next door. Stayed after dinner to watch the Brazil game – We ended up in a tie with Paraguay. Didn't get a lot talked about because Cilene kept butting in. God, that woman has so much to say without actually saying anything at all... I finally just got up, set a meeting for just Oseas, Alberto and myself for in the morning at 7:00 at the church. I am very tired right now. It's

11:30 PM. The day has been long – hoping for a good night's rest.

12/15/99

It's 5:50 in the morning. We are sitting here at the docks waiting for a guy named 'Rigor' to come quote us a trip to Boa Vista. It is a beautiful morning. Promises to be a hot one today. Looking forward to meeting with Oseas.

What a great meeting! Come to find out, the reason this church has not grown and moved forward is the fact that it has never been organized to do so. There has not been a business meeting in over three years. The church, in essence, has had no goals or directive of action in the community. They desire to call Oseas as their pastor, but have been overshadowed by Pr. Elizeu – concerned with "convention" matters of tradition from the denomination, etc. I told them to forget about all that shit for now. Call the faithful members together, now; elect new officers for the church and call a pastor of their choosing; give that pastor Biblical authority and press on as God leads.

As soon as I have spoken to Elizeu, the church will immediately do the above. I pray for God's wisdom in talking to Elizeu. He is from the "old school". Very controlling. He has effectively buried this work. He has become old and ill. God may use him elsewhere, but not here. God, give me grace for this situation. I hate all the dogma that binds the willing from sharing Your Grace with a world in need of it. The only reason the dogma exists is for control through fear and ignorance. I thought Luther had taken care of the question long ago. Fighting such things is what he, (and Christ, for that matter), was persecuted and died trying to eradicate. Can't everyone see that!?. Such utter BS...

Tried and tried to reach Gildo. Sent a message for him to call me about the *Ana*. I'll just send him what money he needs for the repairs already made on the vessel. For me to hire a boat from "Rigor" to take me up there and still risk missing him, will almost pay for the repairs themselves. I've changed my return home plans. Didn't know all the reasons why at first. One main one that has evolved is to be able to head Pr. Elizeu off in Manaus; stopping him from returning here to Barreirinha. I have asked Albeto to come assist the church during the transition we talked about. He will do so. He will also prepare the church to receive Oseas as their Pastor.

We are scheduled to leave for Parintins at Noon today. It is 10:40 AM. Alberto and I have decided to lay here in the a/c until the last possible moment. It feels gratifying to have seen God's hand move so smoothly here. He is in control. I left 2 month's rent on a new house for Oseas to be able to move his children here. I'm sure they are looking around, even as I write this. Just like Christmas for them, I'm sure. I will be telling Richard that we need to build a house for them at some point in time. Either we build one next year or buy one that is adequate for this family to live with dignity – whichever is cheapest.

Well, it's 12:05 here aboard the *Tocantins*. They just cranked the engine – It's packed with passengers this time around. Yesterday, we had 14 aboard; Today, 22. Boat # 7 of the trip – Brings the little game to 2 comfortable and 5 "tolerable, at best" – Oh well. At least it *should* be the last one for a while... It will be airplanes the rest of the way home from Parintins. I've got just enough alprazolam to get me to a pharmacy in Santarem. All is well...

Arrived in Parintins at 5:00 PM. Reconfirmed my flight; got Alberto a boat ticket home; Got me a little room at a place that rents "little rooms", of course. Very decent place. Had a good, long talk with Dad on the phone about the events of the trip. He seemed as pleased as I am with the results.

Talked to Vic. All is well at home. I sure look forward to getting there. The only thing left on the agenda is to speak with Pr. Elizeu about his future role in the work – God give me patience and grace...

Alberto and I had another good fish dinner tonight down the street (Tambaqui Ribs). It was delicious!

Well, it's been another long, hard day. Tomorrow promises more of the same. It is 11:30 PM.

I've had the beers that were in the little fridge here in the room. Hadn't planned on doing it. But, I'm feeling recovered now. Feeling good enough for just a couple.

12/16/99

I am now sitting on the upper deck of the Parintins "International" Airport, awaiting my flight. Had a good night's sleep. As soon as I hit the ground in Manaus, I'll be going after my ticket for home! Hope it's all there for me. In speaking with Vic last night, there may have been some confusion about my departure date. She may have booked me for 2:30 *this* morning instead of tomorrow morning. We will just have to wait and see when I get to the Manaus airport. My goal, after visiting with Elizeu, is to just get home. The time is right...

My cell phone has been off-line since I arrived here at the airport. My flight has been delayed until Noon. I was scheduled to leave at 8:40 this morning. I have tried and tried to get through to Vic to let her know all is well – cell signal comes and goes too quickly to get a call off. So, I've had some drinks – quite a few...

Finally decided to try calling Pr. Elizeu. Unbelievably, I got through and spoke for about 20 minutes before the signal vanished and shut us down. He will be at a couple of different hospitals all afternoon today, running tests. Good thing I got through by phone. What a sweet conversation. God had already worked out my concerns. Elizeu does not want to return to Barreirinha! He desires to work close to home (Manaus). His health is deteriorating rapidly. I really think he just desires to go "home". He has been losing ground ever since he lost his wife a year ago. I told him to call Barreirinha today, officially relinquishing power over the work there, giving full authority to the church to proceed as God's Holy Spirit leads. He will no longer interfere. I also told him *not* to return there. His health and proximity to family is much more important at this stage of his life. He will not return – The church is free to choose and do as God leads. Praise God for that... I believe we can now begin to gradually reduce his financial support, eventually ending that obligation. I will consider this over the next few days. I am greatly relieved. As soon as possible, I need to reach Alberto with all this new news. It has been a matter of earnest prayer over the past days we've spent together.

Just got to Manaus. Called Buck Edder. He has postponed his fishing trips until October of next year. It will hurt a bit financially right now, but at least I don't have to worry about it for a while. I really don't want to do that kind of trip anymore. However, I will stay true to my word on these. When I closed the fishing business a few years ago, it cost me dearly. But, I felt it was necessary in order to salvage me and Vic. Yachts, alcohol and the money seemed attractive, in principle. However, the reality of those years was far different. So grateful to be rid of it all right now. I'm drinking far less these days, than I was then. That's why I agreed to Bud's trips in the first place. Maybe it's time to re-start it, slowly. Very slowly...

12/17/99
I'm finally onboard my VASP flight for home. It's 2:30 in the morning. I arrived in Manaus at 1:30 in the afternoon of what seems like today but was actually yesterday.

The days, boat rides, people to see and issues of this trip, finally have begun to catch-up with me as I begin to relax. I checked in at the Lord Hotel at about 2:30 in the afternoon. Took a hot shower (a first in 11 days) and drank all the beers in the fridge. Last thing I remember is an HBO movie starting at 4:00 PM. Slept all the way to midnight!!

All is resolved, or at least well on the way to resolution. Praise God for it all. The miracles that occurred over these days are without number. God's Holy Spirit was always at least one day ahead of me, preparing the way for me. All the burdens about the work that were with me at the beginning of this trip were, one-by-one, lifted and resolved by God's grace – I was just present to witness the whole thing.

As I look back, had someone like me *not* come, the problems worked out, would still exist. All the issues would have been addressed from a "religious", "denominational" viewpoint. There would have been "pastors" fighting to retain control of people and situations in ghastly, earthly, prideful ways – nothing of God in the mix. I *absolutely hate* the religiosity of this crowd I have to, too often, deal with. I'd rather die a drunk if becoming one of 'them' is what it takes to survive...

As it all unfolded, God acted in beautiful, graceful strokes to smooth the wrinkles that were present. He had me along just to show me how He is able. My trust is all the more in Him. I thank Him for letting me be a part of His plan; For allowing me to witness his Sovereignty up close and personal...

I was drunk when I arrived home. Vic did not pick me up at the airport this time. I hired a car instead. The trip usually takes no more than 4 hours. With all my 'beer stops', it took seven and a half...

Baby, Hanna & the Pool...

I don't remember arriving at the house. When I 'came-to' the next morning, I was told I had walked in the front door, and proceeded straight to the pool area, urinating myself all the way. En-route, I had grabbed "Baby" (our 110 lb. rottweiler) and pulled her in for a swim. As one might imagine, things were destined to became more complicated at home.
Vic was gracious enough to let me stay through the Christmas Holidays, under the condition that if I felt I had to drink, either she and the boys, or I, would move

out to our farm in the country until I travelled again. Needless to say, I spent a couple of months at the farm... I was unable to recognize I had any kind of serious problem around my drinking. I had had a relatively alcohol-free trip this time – at least by my standards. I had not sought out any of my lady friends or committed any other, serious missteps that I could remember. Rather, I had spent substantial time with "men of God" and felt I knew that it was just a matter of 'unconfessed sin'. I had confessed all these sins to God. Now, it was up to Him to forgive and fix me. Or so I thought...

My perception to the "local church" was also beginning to change. I was starting to feel there were too many of them as it was, and the fruit of such numbers was producing more confusion than good for the people we were all trying to help.

I was also beginning to view "missionary activity" as something that needed changing. We should be about sharing the Gospel and nothing else. If the motive behind 'going' was to just establish another denomination in an area, we should stay home. However strongly I feel this as true today, I was in no shape to confront any of these things that troubled me. So, I just drank at them...

CHAPTER THREE

A 'double agent' joins our staff. Can't think of any better reason for having a drink...

This is of the first official trip of the 2000 Season. It is also the beginning of what I call the "dark years" of my alcoholism. I was becoming less concerned about hiding my drinking and more perplexed about why I could not stop. I am officially separated from Vic for the fifth time. By now, I am losing my grip on any remnant of hope I'd zealously tried to hold on to around Vic, my drinking and life in general. But, I still clung to the fantasy of it all somehow going away, resulting in a happy ending. This, requiring little change in me. Among the members of this team was to be a woman I had had an affair with back in 1997. As with all my affairs, this one took place during an 'official separation' from Vic but was the one that cast the greatest doubts in her mind and heart regarding my sanity, work ethic and ability to be trustworthy in any way. It had been my first and only affair with a team member. I had the presence of mind not to ever

repeat such a thing in the 'missions environment'.
I would continue to engage in affairs. Just not at
'work'. The occurrence of these episodes seemed to
escalate and diminish in direct relationship to any
increase or decrease in my drinking. These days,
everything seemed to be on the increase...Vic had
convinced me to hire her brother to keep an eye on
me. He was a good friend of mine as well as a great
task-master. We were happy to be working together,
but resentful of the circumstances that had led to it.
Having Zeek around was like having a "fox
guarding the hen house". We were not about
to do anything to hurt each other. This bought
me some time and gave me a 'dim' hope that
Vic and I might someday get back together.
This Diary begins with the arrival of a team
from Texas, including my father. My Dad seemed
to be an anchor for me when he was around.
He just wasn't around enough, I guess...

Zeek- Died Sober in 2017

FREGUESIA, AMAZONAS
May 22 - June 2, 2000

Tuesday, May 23: The Houston group arrived on schedule this morning. By 7:45 A.M., we were underway. It was so good to see some familiar faces that have meant so much to me over the years - Chuck S., Uncle Howard, Dad... The group, as a whole, seems very tranquil. Fortunately, D was not among them. I heard she might be. Don't think I could handle 10 days out here with her.

D was separated from her husband and I was separated from. She had volunteered to assist me in my rounds on a trip back in 1997. We spent a lot of time together. All was well until we started meeting in the cabin for a drink late at night. The drink. Always the freakin drink. The things I can get myself into with a few drinks and too much time on my hands...

It has been a hectic week here in Manaus making final preparations for the trip and finishing as much of the *Belatis* re-fit as possible. We have literally been up and working, around the clock for the past 72 hours. Looking forward to the next 20 or so of sleep and rest before hitting Barreirinha. God, clear the fog in my brain. I need to think straight. It's been a tough time between trips. I, of course, drank a bit and just feel like dying right now.

Wednesday, May 24: We arrived in Barreirinha at 3:30 this morning. When the sun came up, we hit the streets to acquire the remaining materials to take to Freguesia to build the church. Dad and the construction crew took the *WilPhilMatt* to Freguesia to see what awaits us there. Believe it or not, *nothing* awaits us! We will practically be starting from scratch. Pastor Alberto was to have been here two weeks ago to get things going -- he arrived yesterday. Dear God, hold my tongue...

We finally got things together at Noon. Went through the "furo" (a short-cut) to Freguesia. It saves us about three hours not having to go down to the mouth of the Andira, then up to Freguesia.

As we approached the village, I started to feel at home – excited. I truly love these people and this place. We didn't get anything done today in any of our work stations. Just picked out a place for medical and Bible School. Great worship service tonight. Three adult decisions. This team doesn't seem like 'first-timers at all' but they, for the most past, are. They are taking everything in stride – delays, lack of materials, etc. I thank God for their flexibility. I am slowly, one by one, getting acquainted with those I've never met before, and having a wonderful time rehashing old memories with others. I am very tired. It's been a good start. Tomorrow, the work begins.

Don't feel I need a drink tonight. Maybe sleep her in my hammock. Less of a temptation that way.

As I walked around the village today I couldn't help but remember L walking around it with me. We were both lonely, it was obvious. I don't think either of us would have done what we did if things had been ok back home. What the whole episode did to me and Vic is beyond bad. I blamed Vic for it then. Now, I realize I should have just had more control over the deal. I shouldn't have allowed myself to get close to L. At least not had a drink with her. I'm feeling like crap about it all right now. My memories of things like this get to me sometimes.

Changed my mind. I think I'll go to the cabin and have a couple drinks anyhow. Don't think I can sleep with all this on my mind. Need to flush it all out. Big day tomorrow.

Thursday, May 25: After devotions this morning, everybody hit their location with vigor. Construction was in a *"confused"* mode. Bible School learned *"how to do it"* with Piro (their interpreter) and about 250 kids. Dental plucked and pulled to their heart's content. Wes, our optometrist, fitted a bunch of eyeglasses and did a Pterygium or two. Freguesia hasn't changed at all. The people are, for the most part, very kind, warm and loving.

They still call me "Dr. Bill". I guess when you have needs, you can just pick out a stranger, call him "Doc", and ask for help. I delivered a baby girl here back in 1989. The mother was only 14-years old. This morning, she brought the 'baby' for me to see. She's a gorgeous 10-year old, with curly blond hair. I remember the mother trying to figure out a way to name the baby after me. I also remember telling her I was a newlywed at the time with a jealous wife and didn't need any babies, other than my own, being named after me for a while. We both laughed about that memory today.

Freguesia do Andira

My, my... How time flies.

This is such a sweet people... I have dreamed, hoped, and prayed to be able to bring a group here for several years now. A group dedicated to *this* village. Freguezia has always been a "step-child" of sorts – getting the "left overs" of other towns such as Barreirinha. This time, we are *all theirs*. *"Thank You, Lord."*

We rented a generator in Barreirinha – well, it blew up this afternoon. The power tools were dead in the water. There is a poet that has a "summer home" here and in Barreirinha – Tiago de Melo. He was kind enough to loan us one of his generators to complete the work. We sent Dad to Barreirinha to ask him personally -- his *"Boy Friday"* wasn't about to loan it to us on his own.

Tonight, we had another good service with one adult decision. Made several "house calls" on the way back to the boat. We have absolutely no meds on this trip. I am just handing things with what personal stuff I have on hand, along with whatever the team has to spare. In my experience, God will allow us to do all that He desires to be done here...

Friday, May 26: Whoa! What a short night it was. Several of the team went "gator" hunting; brought back two "huge" 2-footers. How impressive. I guess I'll just have to go one night to show them how it's done…

I had some really strange dreams last night: Donald gave me half of his company and Vic was glad to see me when I got home to Vitoria. My goodness! Come to think of it, both dreams are pretty much equally unrealistic.

Today's work went smoothly. We're going to miss Dad's devotionals when he leaves in the morning. The *Patrice* is just about ready to sail. It arrived here "sinking" from the Tapajos River area. Old Lucifer and his bunch were kind enough to deliver her to us in as bad a shape as possible. Just par for the course, considering.....

Getting to know the individuals on our team better each day. It's a fine bunch. When we first arrived here, nobody had been designated to any station other than construction. Suddenly, when asked, we had Bible School taken care of, dental assistants, the works. God puts these teams together perfectly. He puts an individual in every position that needs somebody.

Things kinda "normalized" for me, too. My head is clearing, and my hands have stopped shaking enough to not be self-conscious about it. Yesterday, my Uncle Howard saw them trembling and jokingly suggested I might could use a drink. If he only knew… The alprazolam I prescribe for myself helps with the "shaking" but adds to the "fog". What a miserable mess…

As I walk to and from the boat/clinic/Bible School/ construction, I am stopped an average of five times by someone or other. Freguesia has always been this way. It is a very trying town, but the rewards are great. Zeek, my brother-in-law and manager, went into Barreirinha today for a couple of things, and called his wife, and mine. All is well in both places. *"Thank You, Lord.."*

I hired Zeek at Vic's insistence earlier in the year. He's a good friend and confidant but has already confided in me that Vic asked him to 'keep an eye on me' and 'report back to her'. After a bit of thought on the subject, he and I agreed to keep what happens in the Amazon, in the Amazon. Largely because he is capable of behavior *far* worse than mine. Never though that Vic would resort to such things. What a bunch of crap...

There was a lot of noise outside the building tonight during the church service. Some kid were throwing rocks on the roof of the pavilion where we were meeting. I'll deal with all that tomorrow. Right now, I'm tired. I did another hour of house calls after church. Gave a baby a shot in the butt, among other things. Now, I just need some rest. The group is holding up very well thus far. No illness whatsoever, yet.

Thinking about the "Zeek/Spy" deal right now. Had a couple of drinks with him just now, in Vic's honor. He just left the cabin. I don't know what her motivation is in trying to keep an eye on me this way. Makes me feel like a "bad little boy". I'm not! I'm a grown man that takes care of her and my business, *very well*. She should just leave well enough alone. She doesn't want me to drink? *She* should stop pulling stunts like *this*...

Saturday, May 27: I just saw Dad off. A bitter-sweet moment for me. I cherish every moment I can spend with him, yet I know that wherever he goes, people are blessed, enriched. I should not be so selfish regarding his comings and goings. Nevertheless, as he pulled away from Freguesia in the *Patrice*, he took a part of me with him. I'm not feeling too good this morning. Stayed up most of the night, "drowning my sorrows". Made me all the sadder to see Dad go. Wish he could have stayed longer...

We had no worship service tonight – we all need to "stop" for a while....

Sunday, May 28: Construction has reached the point of "starting early and going late." However, today they just put in half a day. Got all the trusses built – good milestone. Also started framing up the sides. Dental and optometry ran the whole day. Up till now, the clinics have been running at a "steady pace" -- no huge lines, etc. – just no breaks. The days have been overcast to rainy; the heat, bearable. God has been good, as always.

I started helping out in medical today. Nothing big or real fun. But it was a start. If the hands are steady and the mind is clear, I can't very well say 'no'. Helped with a couple of pterygiums and a fatty-tumor. Helping with those big, juicy things. Kinda sick, I know. So, what else is new?

Our church members here have asked us to have services on the shore tonight, instead of the Community Center. Their little hut on the shore has been home to these believers since the beginning. We had a beautiful service -- mostly believers that have come to know the Lord during our brief visits over the past several years. About 70 in attendance, mostly young folks and adults. It was a great time together.

Sabia, an old friend of mine from here, gave me a duck today! I thought it was one that I could have my chefs make up for me in the Tucupi. When I went to get it, I changed my mind. It was their pet! Weighs about 20 pounds and likes to be held and petted. How could anybody eat a creature such as that?? His name is "Sozinho." (Loner). I just told them to keep taking care of him for me, right there at their home – forever...

Well, it's time for bed. It has been a long, but fruitful day. Speaking of fruitful, I have never received so much fruit in all my days of travel – some 77 trips thus far – everything from Mamao to Tucuma. It has been humbling to see these dear people share of what little they have, with a guy the likes of me.

Zeek went off upstream with a guy that wanted to show him some property. When he got back he'd brought some moonshine made from a called Tapereba. I don't care for the fruit itself, but shine made from it isn't bad at all. Who cares about the taste though. The effect is what counts. Gonna try a taste of it tonight.

Monday, May 29: Lots of 'concerned citizens' today and I feel responsible in a big way. The folks felt that due to the rock-throwing incident the other night, we had decided not to include the community in our services at night. Wow... I had to explain that Saturday, we had a night to ourselves on the boat, and last night, we met on the riverbank. Well, we will definitely meet at the Community Center tonight and hereafter.

The leaders here in Freguesia literally wanted to lynch the two boys that threw the rocks. My goodness! I had to really "act" compassionate, but deep inside, I kinda wanted to lynch 'em, too -- in a Christian kind of way, Ya know?

I had a little 5-year-old, tongue-tied boy brought to me this afternoon. By the grace of God, he let medical numb and clip him. Nobody could understand what he said. So, he tended to be a very quiet boy. Well, to make sure he would continue that way, they took two inches off the tip of his tongue while at it – just didn't want to waste the anesthetic already drawn up!

Construction got all the trusses up today! And also got most of the building studded for walls and windows. Good progress!

OH! BY THE WAY, WE DIDN'T REALLY CUT TWO INCHES OFF THE BOY'S TONGUE! I'm just tired and slap-happy right now – think I need either a bunch of drinks or some sleep. Preferably, sleep... The boy is doing just fine and will probably grow up to be *far* too talkative a creature. Probably has too much built up inside him to be any other way...

Construction has a mascot they've been taking care of since we arrived. She is about the ugliest little dog I've ever seen. They named her "Beiju", mainly because they feed her from the tapioca bread, called Beiju, the ladies of the village bring the boys for a snack from time to time.

Bible School has been running the normal 250 to 300 – twice a day. Danielle, Allison, Piro, Bryan and David have worked their butts off all week. They *and* the kids seem to love it. God does His best amongst His children. The seeds being planted here are countless and priceless. In my opinion, The very young and very old are the true mission fields of this world. Everybody in between has heard it enough. Re-telling them seems a waste of time, resources *and* the Gospel...

My body is just beginning to feel better from last night's Tapereba tasting. Man, I need to not drink at all during these trips. If my mind would just stop long enough to sleep without a drink. I have all that alprazolam with me. Just take a few of those, Boyd. Just feel like an idiot. Nobody else on this boat is drinking tonight. And here I sit...

Tuesday, May 30: LAST DAY MADNESS! The clinics operated at a normal pace and were able to attend everyone that was in line. Praise God for that. Construction got all they could get done, done by 3:30 P.M. The siding arrived from Barreirinha at 2 this afternoon. At least, it's here! I have left enough money with Pastor Oseias for a six-man crew's wages to finish the building. Shouldn't take more than 7 to 10 days, at best. I'll try to pass by here on the way down to Oriximina next week and check on things.

We got everything down to the boat by 5 P.M. Danielle cut kids hair till after dark. I've never seen so many 'buzz-cuts' in one place, at one time, in all my life. Looks like a Skin-heads Convention down here on the riverbank!

Tonight's service was very special. It was the dedication service of the new building. No roof, no sides, no floor – just beautiful under the stars.... Several from the community gave little speeches of appreciation. It was very touching. Gene, Chuck, Wes, and Danielle said a few words on behalf of the group. A truly beautiful night. As usual, the good-byes at the shore were prolonged and teary. We were sailing up-river toward Aiaru by 10 P.M. Mission accomplished – thus far.....

Wednesday, May 31: Aiaru is a beautiful place. We went ashore to track down the village president, John the Baptist, and got all the proper permissions and places to work. Then, we sat down with my old friend (age-wise), Sr. Pedrosa, and visited with him for about an hour over sweet coffee and beiju. I always have a good time with him. He was a heavy drinker back in the day. When I asked him how he was able to quit, he said he just decided to stop and did so. "Will-power", he called it. My goodness, I didn't dare tell him I'd done *just that* more than a thousand times. He must be a better man than I.

Oh, before I forget, I bought a beautiful piece of property on the beach in Freguesia yesterday. Probably as place for me to grow old, *alone*. Good land – good buy.

Back to Ariau... It was a pretty mellow day today. Dental, optometry and Bible School ran at a steady pace. Allison felt a bit of a sour stomach this afternoon, but by evening's end, she felt much better. So far, we've had serious illness among the team members. Thank God for that.

We had a great service tonight. Piro and I "kinda" preached the Word to the people. They were very attentive. The people of this community are very reverent and respectful. I just know the Lord is leading me to start a work here. As He leads, we will go.

All that talk with Pedrosa this morning about drinking has made me want to drink! Just took a couple of alprazolam. Going to try to sleep. Need to slow down with the drink. Don't know why the urge comes so strongly at times. Usually at the *wrong* time. I just need to be stronger. That's all. Stronger. God didn't make me to just be weak like this. I need to do what Pedrosa did. He just stopped. Just need to stop...

Nature Walk...

Thursday, June 1: It's 8 A.M. right now. The group is out on a nature-hike. It's pouring rain and I bet they're *real* happy trekkers. I'm sitting here trying to feel better. Didn't drink last night. Took an alprazolam the minute I woke up this morning. Took another one just now. Hope it kicks in soon.

Crowds were down a bit due to the rain this morning. Believe me, it will pick up this afternoon. Everybody is so tired right now.

The extra two days of work is just not good. We haven't had anyone sick -- but, we're on the verge of losing several. I can feel it coming...

The afternoon went well. Dental had 24 patients in just two-and-a-half hours. They got it all done, though, and nobody was left in line. We pulled out of port at 6 P.M. to head to Manaus – just in time to run head-long into a storm.

It's 7:30 P.M. now and we are tied off in a cove for the night. Found 3 bottles of wine under my bed from last trip. I hope to be asleep within an hour... It was a great two days in Ariau. We will return next year with more help – in every way.

Friday, June 2: We were underway at 5:15 A.M. Smooth, beautiful waters for sailing. ETA in Boa Vista is 11:30 A.M. We picked up a *"guide"* in Freguesia to show us the way out of here, straight to Boa Vista, without having to go back down and around Barreirinha. A 'short-cut of sorts. What a joke! We learned this short-cut together. We arrived just after noon. Had a good visit with Pastor Gildo while we re-fueled. He last saw Dad on Tuesday. He said Dad was "still breathing." That is always my *first* concern when asking about Dad. Maybe it's just a peek into the future of my own children...

We had a nice afternoon of visiting and cruising. This has been a super group and a very successful mission. They want to DO IT AGAIN, and so do I. I really miss my babies. Phillip will be nine years old on June 10. I don't know exactly where I'll be on that day, but my heart and soul will be right there, by his side....

I've tried to stayed away from everyone tonight. Just want to hibernate and be left alone. My mind has started playing its old tricks on me. The 'thought cycle' of Vic, the boys, solitude and impending doom, is waking up again. It is a redundancy that is coming more frequently now. Just want to get back to Manaus and hide until the next trip. It's ironic that after such a sweet time with all these folks,

I feel hell approaching once again. God, fix me please. Don't think I can make it much longer like this. Just don't know what to do.

> *'Blaming' and 'self-pity' are common characteristic among alcoholics. As our drinking progresses, we must come up with good excuses for it. This phenomenon leads us to great reasoning and justification for what we do: 'If she would only...'; 'If that had not happened...'; If only he had...'; 'If people could just understand...'. These, and many more, become common responses in support of our continued drinking. Vic is at her wit's end. I am becoming more careless and open with the fiascos I generated. I am justifying every 'bad choice' by blaming my circumstances, never myself. I am in complete denial. Afterall, I wouldn't need a drink if everything and everybody would just behave as they should. Alcohol ultimately destroys most every good thing it comes in contact with. Marriages and children are among the most tragic of casualties. I've seen such relationships actually survive and thrive when the alcoholic finally becomes sober, but these happy endings are far and few between. More often than not, the damage is too great to overcome. God is very much capable of piecing lives and relationships back together. However, the 'humanity' effected is often too hurt to even seek such restoration...*

CHAPTER FOUR

"Is there something wrong in what we are doing or is it just the wrong in me that is disturbing? Both, it seems..."
I didn't understand it at the time, but I was beginning to question all human, dogmatic input to what Scripture actually said.

On this trip to the Satere-Maue Indigenous Nation, I am beginning to have doubts about the work the Organization is involved in and who I am in the midst of it all. What I saw and internalized during these days would fundamentally change the way I thought and believed.
My Organization had been, from the beginning, allied with the Southern Baptists Church back in the USA, mainly because I was one of them, their respect for my work was great and they had the most resources from which to draw. I'd 'bucked' enough in our Board Meetings to expand this 'alliance' to include any church group that would agree not to preach their dogma – just come and help the people while sharing the Gospel, only. During this trip, my desire quickened to seek out more Indigenous groups to work with, rather

than the typical non-indigenous groups we'd been helping for more than a decade. In retrospect, this wasn't just a selfless desire to share the Gospel. Indigenous areas offered me the opportunity to 'make the rules' that would allow me to drink. These were peoples that had their own 'substances' to help them along the way. Alcohol wouldn't be as scandalous to them as it was to the outside world. This is also the first time any of my children had been with me on trips. Vic had agreed to let our two oldest come along for a while. She'd sent my sister-in-law (Zeek's wife) to help keep an eye on them. Actually, her presence has allowed me to more quickly break my promise to not *drink during the boys' visit. Even my resolve* not *to drink during trips, fell by the wayside. I am so hungover by the time this Team arrived, there was no way I can possibly make it through on just the sedatives. I will need a drink in the evenings in order to survive...*

FLORIDA TEAM
SATERE MAUE INDIAN NATION
July 24 – August 4, 2000

Tuesday, July 25: The team from Florida arrived pretty much on time. It was good to see everyone. There were a few new-comers, but most of them are veterans. It was good to see my old drinking buddy made it as well...

We departed the Manaus port at 11 A.M. After several days of run-around with Takeda Drug Distributors, Margo gave me buying power for meds. I *really* appreciate his help. It took 2 ½ hours to select, order and receive them, but the wait was worth it. My own DEA license is in the renewal process right now. Don't know how wise that is for me, personally...It has been good having William and Phillip alone with me this past week. They've had a lot of fun. I bought a small, floating house a few weeks ago. Not functional for anything other than a 'playhouse'. They've spent the past couple of days cleaning and painting it. Most of the paint, however, ended up on them! They named it the "WilPhilMatt Club". They love it. Also, taught them how to drive and dock the little *WilPhilMatt* boat. The thrill on their faces was worth it all.

My Cabin Aboard the Belatis

I rather overdid it this week. It all started well as the boys arrived in Manaus. I was determined not to drink at all during their visit. All the determination I could muster, faded away at the airport when they walked through the gate. I sent them and their Aunt off with my driver, Wellington, to have some burgers while I got trashed at the bar on the other side of the terminal. I can't remember a single, waking moment this past week without a beer in my hand. I feel angry right now. Why can't I manage to just not drink!? Why doesn't God hear my prayers to relieve me of all this!?!?! Seems like a simple freakin' thing, for an almighty God. Where are you, Man...

We are now headed down-river, about to enter the Parana da Eva. The group is getting rested after their trip from Miami, and my boys are bored. Already they are asking if we are "almost there?" This will be a *long* ride for them. At least they have videos to watch while I sip on a vodka to start feeling right again. Just a few sips while the alprazolam takes effect.

I have no idea what awaits us in Maues. We will be picking up supplies, and Chief Tome, to take us into the reservation. The Grand Chief (called Tuchaua General) has been reluctant to allow us into the main village. It is election time and he fears that we may be used politically in some way. We will begin working deep in Indian territory, but not at the main aldeia (village). As soon as we get to our first location, I will request an audience with the Tuchaua to try and get us to the aldeia during the latter part of the trip. I believe that with a personal visit, we will be able to work something out. God has it all worked out, as usual, but I just won't know what He's worked out till we get there and start working. It's been a long day, and my boys are exhausted. They insisted on getting up with me at 3:30 A.M. this morning to go to the airport to meet this team. I wouldn't have it any other way. I pray God will give us all health and safety as we chart new waters...

Wednesday, July 26: We arrived at 5 A.M. Pastor Aldemir met us at the port in Maues at 6:30. The *Burtis* boat won't be ready to travel until Saturday. The new motor and shaft must be installed first. So, the pastor will travel with us during this trip. We are now taking on roofing tile, lumber and other construction supplies.

Everyone onboard slept well last night. My boys are excited to be here. Our estimated departure time for Indian territory is 11

A.M. Pastor Jose and Chief Tome are waiting for us just inside the territory, about six hours from here. Several folks from Sao Sebastiao have recognized the *Belatis* here in port and have come begging us to re-visit them this trip. They are the further-most village prior to entry to the territory. It was as far as we got last year. I simply told them we would do what we could. All are so very needy up in that area...

We arrived at the edge of the territory just before 5 P.M. Aldemir and I took the *WilPhil-Matt* to Nova Aldeia, the main Satere Village. It was good to see Pastor Jose Rodrigues and his little family again. He's a Brazilian missionary here, with the New Tribes Mission group.
There were *"millions"* of kids and adults gathering around us to the point that we could not speak nor hear each other clearly.

We hopped into the boat again and pulled about 200 yards away from shore to visit. We soon learned that politics are *bad* here right now. The Tuchaua General is no longer Cazusa. The letter of invitation sent to us last year, asking us to come this year to minister, was written by Cazusa, and was annulled last week... Satan, or something, has definitely established a stronghold in the leadership of the Satere's.

I requested an audience with the Tuchaua. To get to him, I had audiences with two separate under-chiefs. These two were the ones who had signed our letter of invitation last year and are still wanting us to come. I went with these two chiefs *and* the woman equivalent of the Tuchaua of the women, to see the Grand Tuchaua himself.

Well, the only "*good*" thing about the actual audience with the Grand, was the 3 rounds of guarana that we men drank as he talked. Kinda like a peace-pipe. Well, no deal. I stood and listened for almost two hours, as he spoke in the Satere language. I understood

nothing. Only two sentences were translated to me, essentially saying, "*You can't come HERE, but you CAN work elsewhere in the nation with the permission of the local Tuchauas.*" Well, it was now my time, and I responded respectfully, yet strongly, that I felt he was being unjust to his people and that he was arbitrarily breaking a pact that was made a year ago, and that the people in *his* village would receive no special treatment wherever we set up to work. I really wanted to slap him upside the head a few times, too. What an asshole. I guess the guarana was taking effect...

We finally returned to the *Belatis* about 8 P.M. Phillip thought I'd been eaten by a jaguar! Everybody was a bit concerned about me, but all was well. While I was gone, God was at work in the heart of the Tuchaua of Monte Orebe. He had sent a couple of canoes out to tell the *Belatis* to leave the territory. One of the scouts he sent, recognized my brother-in-law, Zeek, from last year. By the time I got back from Nova Aldeia, the Tuchaua was on-board waiting to ask if I would bring a team to help his people. What a deal...

This day has been long, trying, but good. Just tucked the boys in and am sitting here watching from across the room, as they sleep. So good to have them with me. What I feel inside right now is a mixture of pride, protection and sadness. I've put these little guys through a lot. I haven't been present in their lives. When I'm home

I just drink until I fall asleep. I drink day and night. They see it. It can't be good for them. And here I sit looking at them, having my forth gin of the night. What a freakin' mess...

Thursday, July 27, 2000: We were up at 4:45 A.M. to *"spy out the land."* I wasn't feeling very fit from last night's gin, but what a day this has turned out to be. John, Mort and I went in to see the Tuchaua here this morning. A very pleasant gentleman. He literally opened the village up to us to do as we pleased. I've learned that most of the individual villages in the territory are "family" units – this one has about 100 plus members. We enjoyed a healthy round of sapo (powdered guarana) with the Tuchaua, as we discussed the work that will take place. You know, I *really* like this sapo stuff! It tastes like water, but kinda makes you feel good enough to go re-roof the Astrodome or something. A *pot* of expresso in every sip. In my younger days, I'd probably try snorting it. After all, the guarana leaf is a close cousin to the coca leaf. Not quite as exhilarating, but good enough for a rush. A rush is nice, from time to time...

All teams were on location by 9:30 A.M. Bible School had a house full of about 50. The translation was awkward being 3-way – *English to Portuguese to Satere* -- but everyone had a great time, even not understanding very much that was said. Construction team is re-building all the well-houses and the generator house in the village. They finished the most complicated one today.

Everyone is well, but the heat is oppressive. The medical team had a steady flow of patients; everybody that sat in my chair spoke Portuguese. Dr. Stue had to go "3 *ways*" most all day though. Mort and Sherry helped pulled some 40 teeth today, without complications or bleeders.

At 4:30 P.M., everybody just vanished from the clinic. We had no idea where everyone went! For a brief moment, I thought the rapture had happened and only us 'Christians' had been *"left behind!"* Come to find out, no matter what's going on at 4:30 each day, the village plays soccer. However, maybe I'll do a little sacrifice to the "great frog god" on the side -- just in case the Rapture *did* come, and he was the true God after all (ha, ha...).

We had no worship service tonight. Didn't really get anything organized during the day. Pastor Jose will fill in for tomorrow. The Indians are basically pagan. They have very little knowledge of our God and Christ. It is totally new to *them*, which is totally new to *me*. I have never before been anywhere where the people do not know *who* Jesus is. This is different. Very different – rather strange.

I've been thinking a great deal about what we *do*; the purpose of the Organization and my place in it. Being among this people; seeing them trudge along in *their* environment as we trudge along in *ours*; watching them worship *their* gods as we worship *our Own*. It brings me to an absolute knowledge that God was here *long* before I came into their lives. Although He is called by a different name, these people have sought Him in the best way they have known to do, for hundreds of years, and He has responded. As I see it, with a somewhat clear mind now, *Christ* is about the only thing missing to complete the Circle of Deity. I *so* wish we could just pronounce His Gospel and leave these people alone. Introducing "religion" and "dogma" into their lives seems cruel and unnecessary punishment for no sin having been committed.

I shudder to think what will become of them if all these 'pastors' and 'missionaries' working among them, are successful in 'indoctrinating' this tribe with their individual 'brands' of Christianity. We already have the Catholics, Baptists, Assembly of God and the Adventists pointing their fingers at each other in this territory. How shameful it feels to be, even *remotely*, associated with the chaos that will ensue as these denominations begin 'peeing on every shoreline', trying to mark their territory. The ultimate result: the Indians end up worshiping a denominational flag as opposed to the Creator and God of the universe. I'm not sure who the heretic is here: me or all the denominations involved in the 'fight'. I *think* all Christ commanded us to do was to share Him with the world. Not sure *at all* He is behind all this 'finger-pointing' and 'competition for souls'. Just makes me want to have a drink, turn this boat around, and leave...

Well, my boys are having a blast. Phillip has "swimmer's ear" so we've started him on Amoxil. He'll be O.K. in a day or two. We took the 'fearless' on the gator hunt tonight. Didn't even see a lightning bug! Oh well, there's always tomorrow...

During the afternoon, the Tuchauas of four villages above Nova Aldeia came to visit me. They have requested us to work in their area next trip. I told them that the Grand Tuchaua had personally turned me down, stating that we may *not go to* or *beyond* his village. Boy, these guys are upset about this! I told them that it's out of my hands. If the Grand Tuchaua puts it in writing, I'll come to help ALL the villages up here. God will work all of this out, *in His time.*

Ah, Happy Birthday, Vic. Hope all is well with you. Trust your '34' is treating *you* better than my '41' is treating *me*. I know you'll have a good one. Me *not* being around is probably the best gift I could give you. Enjoy

Friday, July 28: Another beautiful sunrise this morning. It took a few minutes to burn the fog off. We had a good night's sleep. The boys tend to sleep very well and very soundly. This kind of life seems to fit them like a glove....

All groups were on location by 8:15 A.M. Construction has just about finished all the roofing the village needed done. I had the chance to peek in on Bible School for the first time today. It was great. The people (just about as many adults as children) truly enjoy all the activities. The missionary was telling me that the Indians express their feelings very accurately through facial expressions – no false smiles, etc. Well, these folks are smiling a lot! They are a beautiful race. Very dark eyes, straight cold black hair. You can tell that there has been little or no mixed breeding with the *"whites"* here. Very pure stock. The children are affectionate. They like to be held and pampered.

At lunch time, the children came out in their canoes and actually swam with us. Yesterday, they came out, but stayed far away. They are learning to trust us. We were humpin' today in the dental clinic. Some 65 teeth were extracted, and most of them were difficult – nearly all tough roof-tips. We worked until 6 P.M. Dr. Steve and crew had a steady stream of patients, also. The people here seem to be much more patient and low-key. There isn't the sense of "panic" about getting to see the doctor or dentist. They just calmly wait their turn. No arguing or dissention. The order of things amazes me. There is an underlying respect for others. The children are well behaved.

William and Phillip helped me today. Phillip held the instrument tray, while William passed out toothbrushes and Advil to the patients as they left. I'm having to watch them closely, as the heat is very, very intense. They come in looking a bit flushed; I sit them down with a bottle of water and see that they drink it all. Then they're off again! I'm so proud to have them here with me. It is amazing what a difference having my family with me has made. I feel less tense; more at home and patient; much more mellow. I would like to have it this way more often – as a matter of fact, all of the time would be nice. I seem to be able to control my drinking better here on the Amazon. Might just be an answer to being more present in their lives. I still drink a little but not all day and night long. Maybe need to schedule longer times with them here. We'll see what Vic thinks about it...

We had a great worship service tonight. It poured down rain just before time to go. The hill we climb to reach the village is straight up and made of solid clay. When it rains, it is as slick as boiled okra. No fatal "climbing" accidents tonight though.

The building was packed. Everybody sang for an hour or so; all we leaders spoke some; Pastor Jose brought a 10-minute message from Proverbs 24. No invitation was given. These are *"baby steps."* The Indians are still getting used to the concept of a *"Messiah."* All in due time -- as the Lord leads......

The boys are exhausted, and so am I. Phillip gave up on the service at 9 P.M.. William stuck it out though. He is the most *"disinterested"* one I have about 'church'. It was good to sit with him in this setting. I often wonder about how these little guys of mine will turn out. I know I'm not the best influence for them. I struggle with things I hope they will *never* struggle with. They watch me vacillate more often than I'm steady. This freakin alcohol deal is what I fear the most for them. If God won't heal me soon, I think I'd rather just die and be out of the boy's lives. This is no way to watch their daddy go through life. Not the example they need. Not at all.

I feel guilt and some shame. None of the other dads they hang around with seem to drink like I do. When I take them to church back home I don't think anyone else there has had a drink before the service. If I were these little guys, I'd be confused, for sure. I need to get this deal under control. It doesn't need to be this way. I'll just be stronger. Have to be stronger for these boys of mine.

Saturday, July 29: Unreal sunrise. I didn't venture out till 5:20 A.M. Big day today. Boats came in from everywhere, with folks from beyond Nova Aldeia. Internal politics are getting uglier by the day regarding our not being permitted to go to the upper villages. Speaking of politics: I forgot to mention it yesterday, but the mayor of Maues came to the village. The Tuchaua didn't even give him the time of day. He virtually ignored him. He stayed about 45 minutes and was on his way. "*White*" politicians aren't very welcome up here. Too many broken promises over the decades. They need to maintain this attitude. There is *nothing* of the "white world" I see would benefit this simple people…

There was a steady stream of patients in all the clinics today. I had another difficult line-up of. I guess the Lord is just teaching me patience. William and Phillip had a fantastic time today. They bought REAL Indian necklaces and rings to take home. They also traded a couple of ball caps for two dug-out canoes to try and take with them. These things are as big as the boys are! They used them as floats to swim with at noon.

Construction had fun today – they built a new out-house for the Tuchaua. The hole was already there, which meant the wonderful smell was, too. They put new walls up and a roof. The Tuchaua liked it so much that he asked them to do another one at the school. What a price to pay for doing good work…. The team is in great shape. All systems on "GO!" No one has been sick, praise God. The boat has been operating smoothly. The Indians have no notion of privacy. It has been a challenge keeping them off our vessel. Other than an occasional "*sneak on and gawk for a while*" kinda guy, we've pretty much been able to keep things under control.

I know it's been good for Zeek to have Soraia, his wife, onboard for this trip but I will think very long and hard before I allow it to happen again. I've kinda lost him this trip: he sleeps late every morning, takes long afternoon naps, and just disappears on land. I know he is trying to show Soraia a good time while she is here, but in the process, his efficiency and dependability has dropped by at least 50%. I cannot have that. Soraia was supposed to help me by look after my boys, but that hasn't happened. Thank God, the boys haven't needed to be *"watched"* at all. They have turned out to be regular little *"river rats!"*

The house was packed again tonight for the worship service. We all about fell asleep before I took the stage. The Indians sang songs for nearly two hours!! Don't get me wrong. All in all, it was a good time. I spoke for a few minutes about 'wrong things' and how these separated us from God and how Christ fit into the picture. All went well. A couple of hands went up when I gave the invitation. I have no idea what went on! The language barrier is something entirely new for me. For the first time in my life, I can somewhat relate to the team members that I lead. I can't remember *not* being able to speak and understand Portuguese. This experience will make me more sensitive in the future.

Well, I'm completely exhausted. It feels good to feel this way. It has been a good experience and I wouldn't have missed it for the world. My mind has finally cleared from the fog the beers I created before the trip. I'm thinking and feeling a little better today. The alprazolam is working it's magic. Thank God for that.

Sunday, July 30: Got up refreshed this morning at 5 A.M. Didn't drink at all last night. Quite an accomplishment. The day began with the usual early morning fog. I was quite cold last night on deck. We're having devotions at 6:30 each morning so that those, who want to, can have a quick swim before going to work. It's a nice touch to begin the day... The boats and canoes started coming early this morning. Tuchaua Evaristo, here from Esperanca, came to me at the clinic this morning and said he wanted me and the whole group at his maloca at 3 P.M. for "something special." I was hoping it might be a few rounds of sapo, but it turned out to be something quite different.

He brought out the sacred tribal paddle, made of *"inga do mato"* wood and is well over 100 years old. It has the history of the Satere's carved into it which was done by Evaristo's grandfather, using pig bones as a tool. This icon is the most important thing that this tribe has. It serves to remind them to protect their land and guarana from the white man and orders them NOT to go out and live among the whites. This people was once very violent, and valiant warriors. So much so, that the word *"Maue"* was added to their name by their peers, meaning *"evil"* or *"mean."* The river is named after them and the city of Maues was their first settlement some 300 years ago. What an interesting afternoon.

Evaristo

The paddle told a story of the creation of the world, a flood, spirits coming to earth to persecute the people, etc. The story, which has been handed down through oral tradition for more than 600 years, eerily parallels our own *Biblical* accounts. God was truly already here before religion was introduced. God is inherent in our very nature. What a relief to know. What a simplification to all the chaos man can produce around the subject. The chaos is *not* of Him...

My boys bought lots of Indian necklaces and trinkets, etc. They had a blast! Construction built the out-house for the school. Now the children won't have to walk so far when the *"urge"* hits them during their studies. There was a soccer game across the river today. So, our teams took the afternoon to rest. Mort, Sherry and I decided to keep 'plucking' around at root-tips. We worked till after 5 P.M.

Tonight's service was very nice. Not as many present due to the tournament. A short service and we were home by 9 P.M. Pastor Aldemir preached from Exodus 3:7-9. Did a super job. It was good to just be a spectator for a change...

I had a nice visit with Dr. Stuey this evening out on the bow of the *Belatis*. He's a good man and I enjoyed getting to know him better. He and his teenage son were on last year's trip, also.

Now, it's 11:30 P.M. and I'm beat. I don't want to be awake right now. The whole "ancestral paddle" thing was good for me this morning. Can't seem to get the correlation between what God showed *them* and what He's shown *us*, out of my mind. It has had a great effect on me, on deep levels. Have no idea what these effects are, exactly. Almost afraid to know. Might just change *everything* in my heart and mind. I'm not well. The alcohol and sedatives are keeping me in a cloud. I want to explore what God may be showing me about His relationship to this people – His relationship to all of us. Don't need a big 'change' before I quit drinking this stuff in my cup, as I write this. Seems too deep and profound for my mind as it is right now. My, my, my...

Monday, July 31: It was a fitful but short night for me. I was up at 4:45 A.M. to get my head on straight for the day. Pastor Jose and his wife and their 3-year-old son, Emanuel, have been on the boat with us all week. This child is spoiled rotten. I think it may go deeper than just spoiled though. I'm almost inclined to think there may not be enough pigs in the Amazon Valley to hold all the *"legions"* that possess this kid if they were to be commanded out of him! This little creature is pure evil. Hahaha

A bunch of drunk Indians from last night's party came to clinic today. The party went on till 7 this morning. The Indians here, in general, don't drink alcohol. But the Mayor of Maues, from time to time, sends liquor for them to have a party. Indians don't hold their liquor very well – something to do with their metabolism, I think. Kinda 'kindred spirits' to me, maybe...

Anyway, these guys weren't feeling well as the alcohol began to wear off. I know *that* feeling well... Anesthetic isn't as effective when a guy is drunk. There is a time to numb the flesh and a time to numb the soul. I guess these guys just learned that if they numb the soul when it's the flesh that needs numbing, things don't always work out very well...

The team went on their jungle walk this morning. It's always fascinating for our *"Gringos."* William and Phillip went, too, and brought back all kinds of leaves, medicinal sticks and stuff to clutter up the cabin with (ha-ha). They are going to end up with a pretty impressive *"Show and Tell"* to take home! In the meantime, I went up to talk with the Tuchauas over a round of sapo. They gave me the letter of invitation, drafted and signed by 13 Tuchauas, requesting that we bring more groups to the territory. They have also drafted a letter of invitation for the Grand Tuchaua Antonio to sign. They really sounded like they were going to *"nail"* this guy. Tuchaua Cazusa, and 3 others, will leave tonight to take care of this matter. It's in the Lord's hands, completely.

We didn't actually start working until after lunch. The crowds were small, so it worked out very well. Construction finished up, completing all there was to do. They closed in the last well-house at 5 P.M. Medical left no one waiting in line; dental had to work till 5 P.M. to finish all *our* line. It ended up being a good, long day, after all...

Our *"farewell"* service tonight went on till after 10 P.M. Tuchaua Evaristo thanked us on behalf of his people and himself; Tuchaua Cazusa said a prayer of gratitude to God for sending us to his people and prayed for our safety as we travel tomorrow, and for our quick return. I thanked them for their hospitality and patience. John did the same on behalf of the group. A truly beautiful time on shore tonight.

I marvel at how God has *totally* opened the hearts and minds of these Satere-Maue Indians, to our presence here.

It's quite late now. We reflect on this day and all its blessings. The boys are tucked away -- it's midnight. I've been sitting in my cabin, thinking about all that's happened on this trip. So much to sort out in my heart and mind. Just finished the last of my vodka. Didn't have enough left in the bottle to numb me. Maybe shouldn't have even started without enough to finish. Like it or not, it's time to call it quits for today...

August 1: Up at 5 A.M. No early-risers in this group. The first sign of life came from the hammocks as they began the treks to the bathrooms at about 6. We *planned* to leave no later than 11 A.M., after the clinics had seen all those waiting in line. Everything and everybody *but* the team was onboard and ready to go by then. I went for a farewell chat with Tuchaua Evaristo -- a great visit. He gifted me with a necklace he was wearing. A very special event. Pastor Jose told me later that a gift from Tuchaua to Tuchaua was very special indeed. One more little treasure to remind me of our time here...

William lost his camera – bless his heart. He didn't have many shots taken. He was afraid I would be angry with him. I just held him awhile and all was *ok* again. It is now 2:45 P.M. and we're making good time. The last time we made this trip back to Manaus, we limped along at 1000 RPM's due to a chipped prop. There's a *big* difference cruising at a steady 1500 RPM's... We will drop off John, Jack, and Mort in Maues. Piro, one of our interpreters, will stay with them, and they'll be visiting up the river between this trip and the next. Pastor Jose will also accompany them. I feel comfortable with their staying and visiting in the tribal villages. The Tuchauas will care for them; they've grown to respect me in the past days, so I'm confident they'll care for my people in my absence.

I called Vic and we talked several minutes. All is well at home. She quit her job today. I felt great joy in her being out of the grip of that environment, but the reality of my being the sole provider now kinda hit me, too. I know the Lord will provide. I am faithful to Him, and He is faithful to me. Vic has been so fiercely independent over the past 4 years. So, this will be a big change for our family. I pray she will accept *"being a mother"* as her calling in life for a while. We *all* need her at home right now...

Wednesday, August 2: Estimated time for arrival in Manaus is set for 10 P.M. It's been a good day of rest and reflection for the group. I've had an opportunity to visit one-on-one with several. Our *"share time"* last night was inspiring, as always.

My boys are not looking forward to getting back to the normal *"grind"* of school and city life. Who is, for that matter? They are, however, looking forward to their Mom being home with them more. Phillip told me this afternoon that he never had liked her working all the time...

I didn't venture to tell him that her job has done more *harm* than good to our family *in addition* to the fact that Mom was never home.... The job, and the people related to it, has caused more stress than joy; more debt than income; more division in our home. I know I tend to drink too much from time to time. But, *her job* has had a lot to do with my drinking as well. She blames my drinking for most everything bad that happens. She is *just* as much to blame as anybody. A lot of the time I just drink so I don't get upset at what *she* does. Maybe this is the answer to it all. Thank God the job is out of the picture now. We'll have to see how it goes.

Thursday, August 3: This has been truly a beautiful trip. God has deeply and richly blessed. He has kept us all healthy and safe. He has allowed us to reach a totally new people in His name. He has allowed sweet fellowship among the group. He has given William and Phillip the opportunity to taste the Amazon Valley and to see what the work of their Dad is – What keeps me away from home for long months at a time...

I am desperate here. I want my children to be physically closer to me. The things God is trying to show me are obscured by the effects of alcohol and sedatives. On some level, I am aware of something that should be taking place in my heart and mind, something my drunken lifestyle is inhibiting.
I am becoming more able to shift the blame for my circumstances on to Vic, or just about anything else that might be a passive target. I am now trying to blame her for the misery and confusion, something she had always blamed me for.
As I have reflected on these words I wrote, I can see the whole new dynamic God was trying to introduce in and through me. I was desperate to seek and know Him. I wanted to understand the things I was seeing and feeling. I wanted something in my world to make sense. I simply didn't know how to bring this understanding about. With this conflict between what I saw and what I should be seeing, ever growing, the easiest solution was to drink over it.

CHAPTER FIVE

'If I really loved Vic and the boys, I'd simply not drink'. A more untrue statement has never been made. I simply didn't know how <u>not</u> drink...

I've just sent my boys home to their mother. I am remorseful, angry and baffled by my seeming inability to keep even the smallest of promises and commitments made to Vic, God and myself.

The curiosity and questioning that began on the first trip to the Satere's, is now intensifying. My reaction and posture towards God, is becoming more confrontational and pathetic. I question His love and authority over my life. He isn't behaving 'properly' towards me. He ought to be 'helping and healing me', not just sitting back, watching as I crash and burn...

We are returning with a fresh team to the Satere Nation, just a week after leaving it. I am attracted by the Tribe's simple ways. Intrigued by their relationship to God and each other. Their isolation and obscurity is attractive to me...

COLORADO TEAM
SATERE MAUE INDIAN NATION
August 7 - 16, 2000

August 5: I'm sitting here on the upper deck of the *Belatis*. It's quiet except for the sound of the generator below deck. I've been drinking since the Florida team left a couple of nights ago. So much noise in my head. I feel guilty that I wasn't available to the boys while they were here. Vic is pissed off at me for the drinking I did after promising not to. I don't want to be doing this work, but I don't know how else to live my days and provide for my family.

I truly don't know what to do. These past days, I've just drank and slept and drank and slept. Zeek has had to manage the turning of the boat by himself. I just hope he hasn't overspent the budget. I really don't give a crap though. The noise in my head has been overwhelming. All the voices are mine. So, I know I'm not *totally* crazy.

Just don't know how much longer this can go on. I feel my mind and body slowly dying. I'm too young for this crap to be happening. Not much I seem to be able to do about it though.

Why are You not helping me? Why are you just sitting there? I gave my life to You long ago. I feel abandoned. I feel like You don't give a shit about me. I've tried to live like I know You want me to live. It hasn't worked. Here I sit with the only thing that calms my mind and body. Yet, I know you don't want me to be drinking it. Well, show me something different then! Relieve me from this hell in some other way! Why do you just sit there all high and mighty! Do something, please...

August 8: What a trying day. The Colorado team arrived at the Manaus Airport at 5:15 A.M. I'd been up all night. We lost three interpreters to the bars last night, so I fired them at 2:00 A.M. In all fairness, I guess

I should have fired myself as well. It all worked for the better because by 8 this morning, we had two new ones – both Christians for a change. Maybe we won't lose these to the bars as quickly...

We got back-ordered on medicines again, but we have more than enough to run this trip.

Leaving Port

It's great to see Dr. R again! He's the only veteran and he brought 17 first-timers with him. It's going to be a beautiful trip for us all. My heart was heavy as we pulled out of the Manaus port. It was so very nice to have had William and Phillip with me the past few weeks. It was sad to be heading out without them; the memories still so sweet and fresh on my mind.

I got a call from Pastor Jose this morning about 9:30. Thank God, Dad called about the same time. It seems we need a letter to FUNAI (Indian Bureau) explaining who we are, etc., for entry into Indian Territory again. Dad wrote the letter and faxed it to the Bureau Director in Parintins, so that permission will be awaiting us in Maues when we get there in the morning.

Man, what a first day... We finally got fueled and pulled out of port at 11 A.M. Vic called to say farewell -- she sounded kinda sweet, considering. It usually helps me to hear from her before heading into the bush. Even when things are not quite right between us. She didn't mention my drinking. That was a blessing in and of itself... Well, I am beat. It's only 7 P.M., but I'm ready to say good-night. No alcohol in my cabin this time. I sort of wish I hadn't decided to do this. But, I know not having it in the cabin is the best way to go.

Wednesday, August 9: Unrestful sleep last night – I kept waking up every hour or so until now, 5:30 A.M. The sun is rising beautifully. I'm having alprazolam and coffee for breakfast. Should be feeling better in a bit.

We lost at least an hour, early this morning, when the belt on our water pump broke. The engine shut itself down before overheating. Thank God we carry spares parts now!

Since we haven't yet reached Maues, I'll take this time to express my concerns before You, God. Before I do, please forgive me for my outburst and complaining. When I drink, I get angry because I'm drinking. When I don't drink, I get angry because I'm not drinking. Just help me, please...

I have concerns about my family. With Vic not working, we *must* cut our budget way back. I'm concerned with all the additional costs we have had on and between trips this year. The trips have cost about 25% more than I had planned , largely due to the exchange rate. Between trips, we have kept pretty much a full crew working and have continued to invest in improvements. This has been much needed, but it has cost so very much.

So, Lord, I'm Yours, Vic and the boys are Yours. This vessel is Yours. This ministry is Yours. Continue to teach me to be a good steward of my time and Your money. Continue to comfort and lead me in the paths You would have me to follow. Remove from me the anxiety that comes from time to time and messes things up. If I wasn't certain You can take care of all this, I don't know that I could carry on. Just give me strength and grace to keep going, please.

We arrived in Maues at 6:30 this morning. We hit the ground running. Picked up our three "missionaries from our last trip" up here. It was great seeing them alive and well!

My drinking buddy was obviously "smooth". He even brought me a "gift" from shore. I'll just put it away and try to forget it's here. Sure wish he hadn't brought me a bottle. I was determined to make this trip without alcohol. It's going to be hard to keep it hidden away and out of my mind. Damn...

Zeek spent the morning collecting supplies. I was in meetings ALL morning with officials from the Health Department and Amerindia (FUNAI's legal branch). Finally, after several hours, we had all the paperwork we needed to get underway. FINALLY, we have all the official "permission" necessary for entry to the Territory. Time to set sail.

We set out for Mount Horeb at 2 P.M. We had another good orientation meeting on the way. This is such a fine group of people – surely they're Colorado's best! We will be running a very basic clinic on location, along with busy dental and optical services, Bible School and evangelism. I've been told there are few Christians there.

Well, it's only 8 P.M., but I'm laying it down anyway. A good night's sleep will help clear the cob-webs.

Thursday, August 10: I slept extremely well -- *all night long*. I've needed a restful night for several days now. I got up at 4:30 A.M. The sunrise was breath-taking. We left for shore at 6:30 to set-up locations and all teams were in place by 9 A.M. Construction will rebuild the Health Clinic as well as a couple of out-houses.

The medical clinic started out with *too big* of a "bang". I met with everyone at noon to try to slow things down. The Indians here are slow to arrive, therefore, no a "mass-production" type of arrangement is called for. My concern was simply that my group not wear down too quickly, and not get any more results than having worked at a slow pace. The Health Agent, Saaba, and Pastor Jose went out to line up the surrounding villages for attendance over the next few days. Isaias, the Tuchaua here, has been very helpful. He and I hit it off on the right note when we shared "sapo" and some dried ants together. Just what I needed...

It is good to have the two J's and Mort back with us after their "between trips" adventure. They are giving good feed-back and helping to coordinate the different work stations. This afternoon should run smoothly. We had one of the group to overheat a bit at the clinic. I think it drove home the "dehydration" message to the rest...

The afternoon did, indeed, go well -- much slower pace. I spoke with Saaba and Pastor Jose. We have decided that there will be only 150 or so people to see in this area. We've planned a move deeper in, to Santa Maria, for Saturday afternoon. The plan is to stay there until departure on Tuesday. Santa Maria has 260 inhabitants. We will be busy there. Zeek, Nonato, Jose and a guide went out to check to see if we have enough water to navigate up on the way up. We do.

Had a sweet worship service on shore tonight. Mostly children in attendance. We sang and sang, and then I spoke for a little while. Once again, I find that these people have a very limited knowledge of Jesus Christ. Everything must be spoon-fed to them.

Even then, it seems that the whole concept of the "Holy Trinity" kinda blows over them. So much about God must be understood purely by faith. Impossible to make earthly sense of all of it. I don't think we're supposed to even try.

I'm seeing that with these Indians, what is not readily understand, is lost. They do not ponder very much over issues that are not absolutely "black or white." The simplicity of this moves me, deeply. The message I hear being preached outside of here is neither "black *nor* white". It seems couched in rules and regulations that I cannot seem to find *anywhere* in Scripture. I have a suspicion that the Indians may be right. Maybe God is protecting them from all the needless "stuff" out there by keeping access to them limited by the government. Maybe this simplicity is actually pure genius in disguise…

After tonight's service, the two J's and I were invited to an "Ant Ceremony", about 20 minutes from here in the *WilPhilMatt*. What an incredible ritual! It is the initiation of a boy to manhood and involves an all-night deal of sticking their hands into a glove filled with poisonous ants (called the Tocandeira ant), and dancing and chanting. The three boys being initiated were about 10 to 12 years old. The venom of this ant is equal to that of a scorpion. There are dozens of them inside this glove. The pain, dancing, and chanting will go on until noon tomorrow. I pulled Evaristo over and got the "story" about what I was seeing. The Paje (witchdoctor) is the one who places the glove on the boys and determines how long they will keep it there before joining the dance.

The young girls that hold hands with the boys as they dance, are there to provide incentive to these little guys. Help them be courageous and not faint from the pain they feel. In the end, these girls are given to the boys as a prize for becoming men. During these ritual, the girls can have sex with the boys without it counting against their virginity when they eventually get married. Just part of the culture. Pretty crazy…

We stayed for a few of hours. These guys were drinking and smoking some stuff I'd probably best stay away from. "Big J" took a couple of pictures, with permission, and then we returned to the boat. Me and my drinking buddy, Jack, just stood obsessing over whatever it was these people were drinking, I think... It's been a night that we will all remember; the chanting was haunting...

Friday, August 11: Another short night, but I was well rested. The Lord continues to give gorgeous sunrises. The clinic was very busy this morning. I had a big meeting with the Capitao Geral (General Captain) of the Satere's. We got the groundwork laid for future trips. There will be: (1) Communication of specific construction needs; (2) Communication of specific population needs for medical; (3) All communications will come via Pastor Jose directly to me. All of these points will be most useful in trip preparation on the part of the groups coming from the USA. Up until now, we've been playing a "guessing game." Next year, we'll know better how to prepare.

Our people are suffering from the oppressive heat. They *must* continue to work, but at a much slower pace. I realized last night, as I lay in my hammock, that this group is having to conquer the obstacles of time zones *and* altitude. They have come from 6,000 feet above sea level to about 80 feet above. Huge physical adjustment...

Today has been extremely hot though we've had some cloud covering off and on. Reminds me of Freguesia on the Andira River. Even with the heat, only a couple of the team needed to take the afternoon off.

The *Burtis* vessel brought several loads of people in from surrounding villages. Lots and lots of people. Our two dentists, Ralf and Pike, have more patients than can be humanly handled. Mort did a great job with medical patients; more than 30 patients were given eyeglasses. We have 38 people signed up for tomorrow morning to see the dentists. Maybe set up a chair and I'll help them. I might enjoy being 'too busy' to be bothered for a while. When you're helping pull teeth or cutting on somebody, most people tend to leave you alone...

The "farewell" service tonight was beautiful. There were lots of people in attendance from the other villages, staying over for clinic tomorrow. It was a great night. Everybody spoke a word or sang a song. The Tuchaua even served two rounds of sapo during the service. This kind of thing could *really* catch on! Well, maybe not with the Baptists...

I'm extremely tired tonight. I've finally broken into my 'gift' from Jack and am drinking it right now. Not sure why I did it. But, it's done. Oh God, here we go again...

Saturday, August 12: Didn't sleep much last night and was up at 4:30 A.M. I received a note from Tuchaua Evaristo last night at the service, asking that I come over to Nova Esperanca this morning to visit him. I really consider him a friend, and not just an acquaintance. We had a great visit, and I was back with the team working at 7:30.

Ralph and Pike had a great time pulling teeth together. It was good to get my hands dirty again. Construction, Bible School and medical/dental/optometry were completely finished by noon, and we were loaded up and underway by 1 P.M.

We are now headed up the Urupadi River at about 900 RPM's. The channel is like a maze -- we cross our own wake at about every turn. Many, many tree trunks all over. We've hit the prop once; have lost about 6 inches off one of the blades. We have some significant vibration, but we're O.K.

We're headed for Santa Maria. We don't know what awaits us there – we just know there will be much need. They have been pleading, begging primarily for dental help. *That*, we can provide! Pike and Ralph are fantastic. The *entire* group is wonderful. Never before have we had "first timers" this gifted, organized, flexible, and loving. Only God could have put something like this together.

We arrived in Santa Maria at 5:30 P.M. Pastor Jose, Saaba, and I went into the village to check things out. This is a *very* large and *very* poor village. We sat with Tuchaua Joao for 30 minutes or so. He's very glad to see us here and welcomes all that we might be able to do for his clan.

When we arrived back at the *Belatis*, the *Burt* had just arrived. Aldemir had been stopped on his way here by some folks from a village near Mount Horeb. There are two ladies there that had some teeth pulled and are still bleeding. I am certain there is nothing to it, but decided to send Saaba, the Health Director, back with some gauze, just to make sure. It's hard for these folks to follow instructions: keep the gauze in for an hour after the extractions and do not spit! I guess some things just don't translate well...

Sunday, August 13: It's 5 A.M. and Saaba hasn't returned yet. I have decided not to go ashore with the group and begin work until he gets back. I need to hear from him, that all is well with the ladies, before we continue. You see, Grand Tuchaua.

Antonio is just looking for an opportunity to lash out at us and those who are responsible for our being here. I have never felt so constrained in an area before. At times this week, I have felt "bound" in what I should and shouldn't do with regard to services we offer to the people. I have *never* felt "general" restraint in helping communities before. There have been the isolated instances within a village, but never in an entire area. After all this is over, God will show me what He is teaching me these days. As always, it will be in retrospect. In the meantime, He will give wisdom and grace to continue -- one procedure, one village and one day at a time.

The Satere Maue Territory is a world of a different kind. Some days, the same "heaviness" that I've felt in Barreirinha, comes to life here, also. There seems to be much warfare going on "in the heavenlies" that I cannot see down here.

By-the-way, we had a great share time last evening. Pastor Jose and his wife shared about the culture and their ministry through the New Tribes Mission Organization. It was very touching. They made some prayer requests and also a financial one. This Colorado team will meet them all. I thank God for dedicated people such as Jose and his family. I thank God for people such as this team that will meet these needs as they are made known. Even though I'm a little unsure of where I stand around the "church", as we know it in the "white world" being established here, I *am* grateful Christ is present, by whatever means.

Saaba arrived at 9 A.M. All is well with the "bleeders." Thank You, Lord, for taking care of every situation. All teams were back on location and working shortly after Saaba arrived.

Construction is re-doing the generator house and building an out-house for Tuchaua Joao. The clinic was hopping, as usual. I don't plan to do any dental at this village. Today is Father's Day in Brazil.

Lord, I miss my family. I know they are thinking about me. I guess it would be true and appropriate for me to confess that today, I just want to go home. I really *do* want to go home, but Lord, You know all things. You know my needs and desires, but I know that I am where I need to be, today. It is here, not there.

The afternoon rounded out and ended well. Medical and dental saw everybody that was waiting. The kind of "automatic shut-off valve" around here, is soccer. The games begin at 4 P.M., and everything in the village stops. The Indian culture seems to have all of its priorities lined up just right: pleasure first, and then everything else... Ralph pulled five of Tuchaua Joao's teeth early this morning. He's been 'quiet and manageable' all day. I think we've found the secret to avoid having to deal with "special requests" for materials, donations, etc.: Just pull the teeth of the leader on the day of arrival, and the rest of the time on location will go smoothly.

Well, it's late and I'm tired. I've solved all the world's problems that I care to for one day. About now, I'm feeling more and more grateful for Jack's little "gift". Hope it holds up for a few more days. If it doesn't, I'll have to make arrangements for more as we pass Maues. After several days of dealing with so many personalities and situations, I feel I need and deserve some relief. I am questioning more and more what I'm supposed to be doing here. Just want to present Christ to these folks, fix their bodies, enjoy their lives and go home. I don't think *anybody* would blame me for having these drinks....

Monday, August 14: When I got up at 5 A.M., I thought about shaving. Dispelled it with haste. After all I drank last night, my face would be a bloody mess. Shaking too bad. Took a couple of alprazolam. Waiting for them to take effect before I venture out into the world.

Today's the last day on location. It's always a day of mixed emotions. It's time for the team to go home, yet there is still some time on location to further bond with the people. Sometimes, when we have visited in more than one village during a trip, I feel it might be easier to leave. In all reality, it is a 'cumulative' bonding that takes place. It is with a "people", not just a specific village. Therefore, it is never "easy" for a group to leave.

It's been a good, last day. All teams were finished and loaded up and out by 4 this afternoon. Our boat crew actually won the soccer game played with the villagers!

The farewell service was moving tonight. I must confess that I came to Santa Maria with the misconception that they would badger us for everything we have. I was *so* very wrong! *God, forgive me...* This village, and its Tuchaua, have been gracious, kind, patient, and giving. They have asked for nothing – so we gave more freely.

I felt humbled. What a beautiful show of appreciation. The Tuchaua and other leaders thanked us, graciously. There was an elaborate ceremony, of which I understood little, crowning me "Tuchaua Bill". Just know that it is an immense honor they'd never bestowed on any "white man" before.

The teacher gave me a woven basket. Tuchaua Joao said kind words. He shared that we are the *first* group that did not come to exploit them. That we were the *first* group to come and do *only* that which we said we would do. We came in Jesus' name, to heal their bodies and introduce God's power to heal the soul. That is *all* we did, and they appreciated our transparency.

Seems everyone else comes to gawk at them, watch their rituals, take pictures, make promises to them, then leave, nevermore to return. It's like these people are treated as freaks or toys to be played with and then toss into boxes along with all the other, quaint memories of these observers. Pisses me off to see this. Infuriates something deep inside me...

It's 10:45 P.M. and we are underway, winding through the narrow channel of the upper Urupadi River, beneath an indescribable beautiful full moon. My mind and heart are filled with a different food tonight. The words of the Tuchaua still echoing in the emptiness of my soul. That soul is being filled with something better than alcohol tonight. Maybe the healing has begun. God, I hope so...

Tuesday, August 15: Up at the usual 5 A.M. We arrived in Nova Esperanca at. The team went on a "Nature Tour" and seemed to have enjoyed it. We stocked Saaba's medicine chest to help his people and gave him 30 roofing tiles to cover the Health Department's building in his village. These are all things that will help our entry here next year.

Due to a bad storm with high winds and heavy rain from "up the river", we were somewhat delayed, and didn't arrive in Maues until 5:30 this afternoon. *Burtis* had left a couple hours before us, so had no problem with the storm.

We picked up a new door for the kitchen area and refueled. We said our good-byes to Pastor Aldemir and Pastor Jose and their families and made some phone calls. I called Vic. She sounded mellow and good. God may be doing something in our lives.

When the trips are over, she and I will sit down and map out what we should do next. I trust that both of us will seek God for the next steps to come. Lately, our choices haven't seemed the best. We've been at each other's throats. We both scream so loudly that nothing can be heard. We hurt each other with words. Devastating to even think about right now.

Wednesday, August 17: Up at 6:30 A.M. Got the team on their plane late last night. They're on their way home. I'm feeling little things, like sniffles, etc., as my body begins to relax – rather common at this stage of the trip season. The body finally saying, "slow down".

Last night, I prayed for my "Drinking Buddy" who, while in Brazil, took a six-figure hit on one of his investment companies. He has such a good heart and love for the Amazon. I am comforted in the fact that God will keep things under control for him.

I took the opportunity to pray for Donald, also, as I do with great frequency. Men with good hearts and generous dispositions are often overlooked in the prayers of others, assuming that they have no serious situations or problems. I know better.

Sometimes, I don't think people pray very much for leaders like me, either. They just assume we are "above" the need of it. As I sit here on my deck again, with a fridge-full to run through, I think not. Surely I'm not alone in this. Surely there are others like me that have struggles of their own. Surely, I'm not the only one living in a broken home with a broken soul, doing this kind of work. If I am, Lord, just take me home to you. I'm done...

> *Other than what was mentioned in the introduction, I see the issue most prevalent on my heart and mind during this trip is the 'nature' of our work. I am experiencing more clarity around the duplicity of denominationalism. I am a Christian, raised and working with the largest Christian denomination in the world. However, I am beginning to resent the teaching of 'dogma' as part of anything I am to be involved with. The Satere moved me deeply. I am becoming protective of their simplicity. All of this is good, in principle. But my lack of direction in how to move forward leaves me with little more than 'complaining' as a reaction. Regarding alcohol, it's mere, unexpected presence is enough to melt any resolve I may have had not to drink it. It is a 'predacious creditor' that needs to be paid. It embodies the only calm and relief I know. A calm that always preceded the tragic storms to come...*

CHAPTER SIX

"My wife leaves me because of my drinking. I drink some more and have an affair. Then I drink a lot more because my wife left me, and I had an affair."
No break in the clouds. Just another hurricane after every devastating storm...

This is the first of two trips back into the Satere Indian Nation. A place I am growing more and more fond of. The questioning about my spirituality is becoming more pronounced in my day-to-day experience of the world around me.
In the Winter of 2000, Vic and I had already split up again, but are open to getting back together. I've moved the family to Dallas, Texas before heading to the Amazon for the Season. Vic thought it would be "healthier" for her and the boys if we were further apart for a while. She was certainly right about that. Earlier in the Spring, I'd had an affair with a young woman named 'B'. It was short-lived, but further confirmed that drinking led to things more complicated than just my drinking. I was beginning to feel resigned to maybe never getting any better than I already was.

> *The key, I felt, was to figure out how to manage the misery while limiting the quantity of alcohol I consumed and when I would allow myself a drink. 'Control' was the missing factor. Surely, it was just a simple matter of control...*

FLORIDA TEAM
RIO URUPADI, AMAZONAS
July 9 - 19, 2001

Tuesday, July 10: The Orlando team arrived about 15 minutes early. It was a breath of fresh air to see both Jack and John again. One of them was detained about an hour trying to resolve the fine he got last year for losing his entry card. The Federal Police here has gotten strict about these things, but they finally accepted a "cash settlement" from him, of course. So much for "strict".

This was a rough week-end for me. The preparations for this trip went well enough, but I found myself missing the boys, badly. I also came to the realization, again, that I am called of God to do this work. I just feel that I need my family to be by my side. That's all in God's hands and that is where I am going to leave it. For now, I've got a trip to run...

Thoughts about the family become too much for me sometimes. I drank pretty steadily these last days. So tired of feeling like I do before I drink and after. If I didn't have so much on my mind, maybe I wouldn't have to drink to make it all feel better. The drinking doesn't seem to help. But, it is the only company that won't require things of me I can't seem to do. I try to be a good father. I try to run this organization correctly. I try to please Vic. None of it seems to be enough for anybody...I bought a new Jon boat – new to me, that is. It's another 40 HP with steering and controls. It should a great asset to the work as we've been needing a second one to tend the *Belatis*. Been needing it for a long time. The *Belatis* is a huge vessel. Takes two tenders to maneuver her safely in tight spots.

We set sail at 7:30 A.M., heading for Maues and beyond. At 7 P.M., we entered the Parana de Ramos. It's raining. But, should be smooth sailing the rest of the evening. I'm hoping for some good sleep, if I can slow my mind a little....

Wednesday, July 11: Arrived in Maues at 2:30 A.M. Not my choice, but my night's sleep/rest ended upon our arrival. The first couple days of a trip seems to treat me this way, but I tend to normalized by day 4 or 5. My head feels too heavy for my neck. Hard to keep it up. No choice in the right now. We  are picking up building supplies here to put up some more outhouses for the Indians. Pastor Jose should be meeting us this morning to guide us into the reservation. We hope we can pull out of here by noon.

This time next month, William, Phillip, and Matthew will be headlong into school in Dallas. I pray God give them courage and determination to take on English for the first time. I know He will... I have the three most wonderful boys that God could possibly give to a man. I am not worthy of such a thing. William is more serious, even lacks patience at times; *a lot like me*. Phillip is the caretaker. He's always trying to be agreeable and keep the peace. He is sensitive, but has a short fuse, also *a lot like me*. Matthew is the mysterious one – subtle mischief – makes us all laugh a lot. He likes to cuddle; *a lot like me*. Well, these little fellows are definitely blood of my blood. God, help me to raise them to be the men that I've always wanted to be. If somehow they can avoid the mistakes that I have made, they'll end up O.K. Sometimes I feel God has skipped a generation of His protection. At this point, I would gladly go unprotected if it meant He would concentrate on them. I know I'm just talking crap. Just feels that way right now...

We headed up the Urupadi River at 11 A.M. – an hour ahead of my estimate. We saw Tuchaua Evaristo just before we left port. He was in town for a medical check-up. It was so good to see him again. On our return down river, we will stop by his village to visit awhile and have sapo with him.

It took what seemed to be forever to get to Santa Maria – nine hours. Oh well, we finally did arrive at 8 P.M. John and I went up to pay our respects to Tuchaua Jose and then returned to the boat for some rest. I really need a good night of rest....

Thursday, July 12: .....and it was a good night of rest. I slept a solid 8 ½ hours. At last, I'm feeling a bit more normal. I was up at 5:30 A.M. Pastor Jose, his family, and the two single missionaries I met last trip, joined us for breakfast.

I awoke with great expectations for the day. The health representatives should be here this afternoon. We will just play the day by ear and see where God leads. As for me, if a couple rounds of sapo develops, I'll be pleased. I prescribed myself a larger dose of alprazolam to help with the shakes this time. Just need to manage till it's all over. Lost's to do this time around. The meds do a lot for the physical stuff I feel. Just wish they helped with the mind and soul as well...

All teams, except dental, were on site by 9 A.M. After much conversation and strategy talks, water pipes began to be laid and Bible School cranked up.

We've had a problem with one of our interpreters for the past two trips now, *"fraternizing"* with the American ladies. Unfortunately, I need to let him go. At 2 P.M., I'll send him to Maues. End of another chapter...

Dental was somewhat busy this afternoon. It's terribly hot here, but all went well with all teams. I had a couple rounds of sapo with the Tuchaua, and it lifted my spirits a bit. We didn't have worship services tonight. Pastor Jose asked that we wait till tomorrow. So, I told the story of the *"Glove Ritual"* and a few other things which seemed of interest to this team of students. It was a good time.

Friday, July 13: Good night's sleep. Good dreams – I just don't remember any of them. I'm taking eleven people – including 3 locals and a deckhand – in two Jon boats back up to a village called Kuruatuba. We've been asked to visit the Clan again. We plan to do Bible School and dental. Actually, I have no idea what will transpire as the day progresses, but I'm looking forward to seeing what God has in store for us today. The group here in Santa Maria will be in good hands with my brother and Jack.

Kuruatuba

LATER: My goodness! What a day. The "five-hour", round trip to Kuruatuba, turned out to be 8 ½ ! All we had time to do was a 30-minute Bible School. On our return to Santa Maria, we wound and weaved our way through the overhang, jumping the logs in our path. It was a good adventure for our passengers, non the less. It's something they'll never forget. If they only realized what a privilege it is for them to be in this place…

Kuruatuba, is one of the most forgotten and desolate places I've ever experienced. It is the most isolated of the 56 Satere Clans. They are also the closest to the Satere Clans that remain isolated, wanting nothing to do with even their own. I'm intrigued by the Isolated ones. Would love to know more about them someday. Next trip, we will spend two days with them with a skeleton crew of medical. I'd love to drill a well for them as well, if possible.

We arrived back at the *Belatis* at 6 P.M. sharp. Had a service tonight on shore. The message was preached in the Indian dialect. It was a humbling experience for me – I have no idea what was being said. I *do* know that Jesus Christ was being preached and that's all that matters.

Sitting here in my cabin, trying to process what I've seen today. Zeek surprised me with a *huge* bottle of dry, white wine a few minutes ago. Enjoying it, immensely. Somehow I know I'll be sorry for it in the morning…

The contrast between the reclusive Clan of Kuruatuba and the rest of the Satere I have come to know, is profound. When Jose was sharing about the Trinity with the folks up there, I saw confusion, almost fear, in most of their faces. I just wanted to stop Jose and tell them, "It's ok! Just forget about everything this guy just said; Call God whatever you want to call Him; You're weren't wrong in worshiping Him in the way you've felt you had to. Now, let me tell him about His Son. He changes everything. That's all you need to hear…

I often wonder if what I am doing is even right. I wonder if I'm just adding to the confusion of others, regarding what I *myself* am confused about. I just don't see where all that I see is necessary. I just don't see why God would make relationship and communicating with Him as complicated as the church makes it out to be. So many of the various rules I run into among the Baptist, Assembly's and the rest seem related directly to anything Christ ever taught. It seems we've considered "what He *might have meant*" above what He "*really said*". Even though I don't feel God's presence like I'd like to, I know the solution to my problems will be easy once I figure it out. It won't come from obeying a bunch of trumped up rules. Of *that*, I'm certain…

Saturday, July 14: I overslept this morning. Took a muscle relaxer, two alprazolam and drank Zeek's bottle of wine. Didn't open my eyes until 6 A.M. Surprised I woke up at all. Spending 8 hours in a Jon boat yesterday was no party. My body feels it right now. My boys would've *loved* it though!

Everyone on the team is feeling good. Only one, so far, has stayed in for a few hours. The construction crew is laying pipe from the existing well in the village, to the huts of each family. They've gone as far as they can with the supplies available.

Everything should get tied in on the first day of the next team in August. We've decided to purchase 25 to 30 depository tanks to supply every two to three houses. This will give these people a reservoir of water when the village pump is not running.

Tonight, we had a good service. It lasted from 7:30 till almost 10:00. Two solid hours of singing… The Indians love to sing and to be sung to. I like it, too. The catechist spoke some very warm words to the packed house, stating that he could feel the presence of God amongst the team members – very moving statements. Tuchaua Jose spoke to his people, making mention of God to them and how they, and he, should recognize all that this group is doing and what it represents to the Satere Maue Nation. It is all a true gift of Tupana (God) to them. Once again, I was deeply moved. Tuchaua has never made mention of God in speaking before his people in my presence. A good end to a good day.

Sunday, July 15: A good night of needed sleep and rest. Didn't need a drink. Just passed out own my own. Zeek went ashore early this morning to buy the fresh kill of the night's hunting party – a Paca and a Capivara. Lots of good meat.

There have been people from Brasilia here for the past couple of days, installing fluoride feeders into the water system. They have criticized our work here; even threatening to have us expelled from the reservation. It causes me mild concern, and I will make a point to meet with the Tuchaua and his counsel this afternoon or tomorrow. If we are lacking in *any* form of authorization to be here, I will require it of them prior to the next team's arrival next week.

There is such a political battle going on within this Tribal Nation's leadership right now. I didn't want us to be at the center of the confusion, but it seems that we are. I ask God for wisdom in my dealings with these issues and with these leaders. I don't want to draw attention to ourselves. Well God, Do you want us to feel comfortable, or do You want us to help these people? I think I know Your answer but tell me anyway – please.

I didn't have much opportunity to work this afternoon. I met with Tuchaua Joao at 1:30, and then John, Jack, and I bought all the artifacts that the Indians were selling. We decided we would buy it all and then pass it on to the team. This way, it saves a lot of work in haggling. No sooner than we had returned to the boat, Tuchaua Rubens from Kuruatuba and the local captain came onboard. We all expressed concern over the Grand Tuchaua's continued resistance to our being here. We decided to call a general meeting for 7:30 tonight.

Due to our pow-wow with the leaders and the community, we did not have a worship service tonight. Would have been totally out of the context at hand. John, Jack, my brother, Zeek and I were honored guests. These folks were decisive! They are extremely grateful for our presence here and the overall work that we do. For the first time, they expressed as much appreciation for the Gospel we bring, as for the physical help we provide. What a relief it was to hear this.

The whole setting was like an ancient *"Raiders of the Lost Arc"* scenario. The lights were very dim. There was smoke in the air. I was just waiting for the whole thing to get ugly and somebody decide to simply sacrifice the weaker ones among us to the *"dim light"* and the *"smoke in the air"* gods! Oh well. Didn't happen. Everyone survived. The meeting went great. We resolved to continue our work and if *anyone* was to be sacrificed it would be those trying to stop us...

Pastor Jose and his wife came onboard and shared the *"Tocandeira Glove"* story with the team. After seeing several of these ceremonies myself, I don't believe this little couple ever has... Had a great time anyway, late into the evening.

Finally, laying the day to rest at midnight. Going to have a drink or two to smooth out. The meeting this afternoon troubled me. It seems we are at risk of being a major wedge in peace and unity among these people. I don't want to be involved in that way. We are here to unite everyone under the common cause of physical healing and Spiritual completion. The meeting today seemed anything *but* unifying. On the surface, it patted my ego to hear their support for our presence. On the inside, it felt like I was being forged into a weapon they might use. We'll have to see where it all leads. For now, I need to relax a while.

Monday, July 16: Awoke to the last day on location – always a bitter/sweet experience. I only got a few hours of sleep last night. My mind is doing fine, but my body is weary. The day progressed steadily. We dispatched one of our "tenders" vessels to take a 7-day-old baby to Maues. The baby's umbilical cord had been pulled off accidentally and was hemorrhaging. She didn't look good – much blood loss. It was clear she needed more resources than we had on-hand. We were able to extracted a number of teeth today. Candice and Linda have worked well with me all week. It has help that they are *also* beautiful young ladies. Sweet dispositions. Always and encouragement to keep working. I know my boys would have fought to the death for a spot near all the blood and guts, just to be close. Something they wouldn't necessarily do with lesser, visual stimulation…

The team gave out bags of clothing today, going house to house. They've also taken and given Polaroid pictures to the multitudes. I like that – it's a good thing.

Tonight's service saw God perform a mighty miracle --- unbelievable by *anyone's* standards. As is customary, we were saying our good-byes. The pastor had a word, I spoke, and John. spoke. Then came Tuchaua Joao's turn to speak. And speak he did! The other night, he had spoken of God for the first time *ever* while addressing his people. Tonight, he began speaking of Jesus and by the end of his speech, he had announced his public profession of faith in Christ. What a night. The Holy Spirit vividly manifested His convicting presence in the Satere Maue Indian Nation this evening. I feel somewhat better about our presence and reason for being here.

I need to let God do His work and just take care of my little problems as they arise...

Tuesday, July 18: Got underway last night after the service. We cruised for a few hours in the name of *"forward movement"* and *"trip closure."* We stopped off for a couple of hours at Tuchaua Evaristo's village. He was still in Maues. The team went on a *"nature walk"* – one of the best *"walks"* is right here. We sent Pastor Jose over to Vila Nova to *"spy"* around on how attitudes are with the Grand Tuchaua about our presence here and to try to find me some guarana *"Sapo."* I'm really more interested in the *sapo* than I am about the Tuchauas attitude... He's going to fall someday. Just let him fall.

We've had many challenges and blessings these past days. Been able to help many people with their health needs, with more accessible water in individual homes, with opportunities to teach hundreds of children through Bible School, and best of all, we've seen the fruits of the spreading of the Gospel here on the reservation. We've faced challenges of criticism and resentment regarding our presence here. But, through it all, we can say, all is well...

Wednesday, July 19: Just got the group off. Jack is passed out across the deck with an open bottle of something laying across his belly. I'm glad for that. I don't like guests around after a trip. Just want to be left alone. I guess I have no choice this time around. He's going to stay between these trips to relax a little.

It's 4 in the morning. Zeek handed me a cold beer, just as the team finished going through the gate, on their way home. Bless him. "On their way home..." what a foreign concept for me right now. If Vic could see me at the moment, I'd probably never be able to go home again. What do I care though? She's pretty much closed that door anyway. I'm pissed of I agreed to let her take the kids that far away from me. I'm pissed off I didn't stand up to her. I'm broken inside over the boys. It feels like I'm bleeding deep inside. What a stinking mess this life is. What a freakin mess...

> Even through my alcohol blurred eyes, this trip produced some experiences and observations that stirred the Spirit that I'd suppressed within me. These new things I was exposed to would serve as the very foundation of belief and action that would, in sobriety, lead me to the 'ends of the earth'. For the first time, I was introduced to the notion that Isolated Peoples still existed. I knew this to be true in principle. But, now, I felt intrigued by the notion. Today I see that God was working to teach me things that would lay the path of my future. At the time though, it just frustrated me more and allowed me yet another reason to drink. I was becoming jaded and unable to see the 'good' in most anything. My life revolved around the next drink. Everything between drinks was growing unacceptable...

CHAPTER SEVEN

"Denominationalism is the culprit. I hate it and suspect God does too. Not even a drink makes me feel 'ok' about it all. But, I'll drink at it anyway..."

God is trying to guide me to simplicity. My mind and the Spirit within me are so clouded by alcohol and sedatives, I simply cannot see the Path to follow...

The Organization and ministry was growing by leaps and bounds. However, my enthusiasm was slipping in the other direction, almost as quickly. I was becoming more and more critical of organized religion while richly benefiting from it. My desire was to go deeper and deeper into the rainforest with our work. What I realize now is, I just wanted to run away...

The quantities I drank were increasing. I'm unsure if it was because of the internal conflict and recognition of my hypocrisy within it, or just the relief of having something to be conflicted about. Regardless, drinking is all I knew that made me 'fit' to face any of it. Alcohol now had a greater grip on me than ever before...

I had just moved Vic and the boys back to the USA. We had been separated for a good while. I'd just *ended a rather open affair with a woman from way in the past. I was feeling down and alone.*

FLORIDA TEAM
SATERE MAUE INDIAN NATION
ON THE URUPADI RIVER
July 23 – August 3, 2001

Monday, July 23 What a hell of a deal… Been here on the *Belatis* for a few days now. Haven't had the energy to move much passed my hammock on the upper deck. My head and heart have been reeling for days. Moving the family back to the USA seems to have been the right thing to do. Vic feels better there, now that we are not under the same roof. I feel better too. Just seems like my boys are all the more distant from me now. Harder to get to if they need me.

The thing with B is over. Never really started, but it's over now. She was a woman from my past, in Florida. We knew each other back then. But, she was young at the time. 17 or 18, I guess. I had never considered her in any way but a "little girl". Her dad sold me cars back then. Well, 20 years later, she shows up on a trip a breathtakingly, beautiful woman. It wasn't just her "looks". It felt like I was home again, in more innocent, stable times. I know I hurt both these women – Vic and B. I know I should have left the opportunity alone. Don't know how I get into things like that. Actually, I do. Vic tells me to leave, *again*; I drink; I drink; I drink; stuff like this is what happens. I hate myself right now. I hate alcohol and all it does to me…

God, *where are you?* I really don't want to go through this again. I truly just want a happy family. I don't want the distraction of another woman or another freakin stooper. The way I feel inside isn't how I want to feel. I ask you, *again*, to fix all this. I'm lonely.

B was never in my heart, but she needs to be removed from my mind. Care for my family. Love my boys for me. Give Vic a change of heart... I have to stop this craziness. My body is weak. My mind is shit. My spirit is dying – I *know* it is... I know you could adjust all this in the blink of an eye. Please, just do it...

Wednesday, July 25 The Orlando team arrived at 4:28 A.M. yesterday morning. All went well through customs. It was great to see old friends from trips past. I look forward to seeing all that God is going to do through this group and what He is going to do in me.

This week-end between trips, spent with Jack, was very revealing to me. It didn't end until a few hours before the team arrived. This guy is about the only guy I know that drinks more than I! there's hope for me, still...Through our times together, we identified the great reality that Evil is on the warpath. Really though, I think blaming Satan for the crap I do is just a copout. Jack wants to blame him for every behavior he feels bad about. As for me, I know what I'm doing. I don't need any greater coercing to make me screw up. I can do it all by myself. My problem is not being able to stop myself *before* the fact.

We are supposed to pick up Pastor Jose here in Manaus today. He is to have an official letter of permission for our entry into the reservation. I pray that it's all we will need. The political situation among the Indians is not very stable right now. Don't know that it ever will be. Just have to live with it as it is.

At 7 A.M.. Pastor Jose arrived at our boat. He has assured me that our permission has been granted to continue our trip. I truly believe that I will need to make a trip back here, and possibly on to Brasilia, early next year. I feel in my heart that we need all official permission documents before next year's trips to this area. For now, we press onward under God's leadership.

We departed Maues at 1 A.M., headed for Tuchaua Evaristo's village. We will probably have services there this evening. All the dental equipment is in Santa Maria, so Pastor Jose will run up there early in the morning to get it.

We got to the village at 3 P.M. I had the prop changed out on the *Belatis* while stopped this week-end. We've increased our speed pretty well. We made the trip to Maues in 17 hours - not bad at all! We'll check the numbers of fuel consumption when we reach Santa Maria.

Thursday, July 26: Slept well last night. The worship service was over early, so we stayed up a little while to visit. This team is a fine group of people.

As I looked around the village this morning, I remember my boys being here last year. I could almost see them coming and going, bright eyes and eager dispositions. What a precious time that was for me. I miss them terribly. Just want them with me...

We had a very full day. All but the construction team had steady work. At least this gave those men an opportunity to see what else goes on during our trips. So many times, the individual teams are so involved in their work that one doesn't see what the other groups are doing.

The dental team had a couple of difficult cases. Perhaps we should limit the practice to simple extractions. We want desperately to help these people, but not put God's protection and grace to the test.

We left Tuchaua Evaristo's village at 5 P.M. and were through the "tree maze" just after dark. I could just feel ourselves losing a prop at every turn, but thank God, we didn't. We arrived and anchored at Santa Maria a few minutes ago. It's 9 P.M. Jack just left the cabin after depositing his stash in my fridge. Don't really want him around during my down-time. I'd rather be alone. I don't feel well tonight. I know it's just the consequence of undisciplined days. Way too much alcohol. The presence of S during that time didn't help things either. She and alcohol seem to go hand in hand. My goodness...

Friday, July 27: All teams were on location, getting settled in by 8:15 this morning. The construction team finally got their first tower and water tank set before lunch. Only 29 to go... Dr. Stuey saw a steady stream of patients. We did very little work this afternoon. The folks from the government (FUNASA) health department came to the village to vaccinate everybody, so we kinda bowed out at 3:30 P.M. This gave us opportunity to have a good conversation with Pastor Jose about a wide range of issues. He is wise beyond his years and I will pray for him as often as the Lord brings him to mind.

Right at 4, all the village men took off running toward the shore, grabbing their shotguns and bows & arrows as they went. My first reaction was that they were after one of mine! Then I saw that the guy leading this "pack of fury" was our own Zeek! Come to find out, there was a herd of wild hogs (50 or more) about 15 minutes upstream from here, and these guys wanted all of them! They only got one pig, but I guess they had fun. Wish I'd joined them. I think the "kill" numbers would have been better if I had...

Good worship tonight. Tomorrow, we will take three Jon boats and 15 people up to Kuruatuba for the day.

Saturday, July 28: We were up at 4:30 A.M. Had breakfast and then were on our way at 5:30. My brother remained in Santa Maria to keep things running smoothly. It's good to have my big brother back with me for a while. We haven't pulled knives on each other during arguments for a while now. Just best not to drink together anymore. It's sad how relationships can change. In the early years, back in Florida, we used to love dreaming "big" together. He's married every girl he ever fell in love with. I'd just be there when things ended for him. He's on his third wife now. If not for the boys Vic and I produced, I think maybe I should never have married at all. I'm not good at it for some reason...

What a day this ended up being! I have rarely ever felt more spiritually oppressed in this work as I did today. Nothing went right. I was really challenged up in Kuruatuba when, what seemed to be a simple extraction, resulted in removing more bone than tooth. The guy's sinus cavity was partially exposed in the process. Damn...

Kuruatuba is a shy, remote community at the absolute "end of the road", about one block north of hell! The people disappeared when we arrived. It was amazing - the village was a ghost town. It was strange indeed.... About an hour after we got there, a few children began to sheepishly, emerge from the surrounding jungle. Come to find out, the people were afraid of us and were watching us from the woods. I was imagining what Nate Saint must have felt just before he was massacred! What an ominous feeling..... Finally, Bible School ended up with 35 children and youth. The young people began to warm up to the group. It was a relief to see. Evidently, this village had received word that we were "not of Tupana" (God) and that they should keep a distance from us. After our botched extraction, they may have been right after all...

We departed from the village at 2 P.M. on the 3-hour journey back to the *Belatis*. We took the young man with the "scary dental experience" with us for Dr. Steve to look at. Also, during the 3 hours, I felt compelled to reflect on my personal situation here.

I made a *"deal"* with God, a simple pact: *"Lord, if I ever become proud or arrogant in the gifts you have given me, then I will quit. If I personally ever hurt anyone with what you've gifted me to do, I will quit. "*

I've tried to be cognitive in all areas of our work so that I might be of help anywhere I might be needed. God has blessed me in this search. At this juncture in what I'm doing, it would be easy to quit it all and just focus on *"trip administration"*. Lord, You've never called me to do anything for the rest of my life.' You have simply called me one day at a time, each and every day of the past 15 years. You have given this unworthy fool gifts and abilities to fill every need that has come along, especially the ability to recognize those things that reach beyond what You allow me to do. So, Lord, who am I to determine when I'm to be content to discontinue, or ready to obey Your next assignment for me. Forgetting the past and the future, just show me this day what You want me to do and by Your grace, I believe that I can handle it, today."

Sunday, July 29: I slept extremely well last night. When we returned from Kuruatuba yesterday, Stuey examined the *"mouth boy"* and said there was nothing to worry about and I took a huge breath of relief.

My back muscles were hurting and spasm-ing so badly that I found it hard to move. I didn't feel like going to church at all, much less leading the service. But I took a morphine tab, had a tiny drink and went to church anyway, and as always, I didn't regret it.

I did little today. Just enjoyed walking around, having Sapo with the Tuchaua and expresso with Pastor Jose. Sweet, sweet times of fellowship. The more I visit with Jose, the more I am beginning to question his motives for being here a bit. Not sure why, just am.

I feel protective of this people and don't want them messed up by "organized religion". Maybe that's it. Just want to protect them from what the "white world" has done to the Gospel. The chaos they are causing in a world that just needs to hear *Christ's* message, not their own twisted additions to it. Yeah, maybe that's it. Will have to give it some serious thought. Feeling critical right now...

The village had a soccer tournament this afternoon. Our group brought *"team shirts"* for each of the three teams. It was fun to watch. I truly enjoyed not working today. It felt awfully strange at first, and then, I just enjoyed it.

I've felt good all day. We had another good service tonight, with as many adults as children present. The attendance has grown larger each night. These people are hungry for the truth. The service lasted till 9:30 P.M. Jose and the two single missionaries shared their testimonies here on the boat this afternoon and they were inspiring to hear. I still have the question of "motive" swirling around in my mind. These people do a good work though their presence here. However, the Gospel had been presented and there are still many elsewhere that have not heard. Why are they still here, building houses and setting down roots? The Indians are vulnerable to their presence. I've seen signs of them wanting to have houses and "things" like these missionaries have. Just can't see a *plus* for all the *minuses* that come to mind…

Monday, July 30: We were up at 6 A.M. on this, our last day on location. We had a good morning. I've enjoyed Dr. Steve so much. This is his third trip with us. He is a dedicated servant of the Lord. Most of the group went on a *'jungle walk"* this afternoon. Those who went to Kuruatuba the other day stayed on the boat. They've seen more of the magnificence of this Amazon Valley than most *all* white men on the face of this big earth! I hope that they realize some day, that they are among only a hand full of humans that have gone so deep into the remoteness of this Valley; *Green Hell*, as my father once named it. They can count themselves as privileged.

We finally tested the water system. All worked beautifully! Except for a few inverted valves, etc., all the tanks began to fill. This is a first for *any* tribe. The have running water, a shower and reservoir tank at *every* hut. Santa Maria will be the envy of the entire Satere Maue Nation. I'm proud for them and prouder of these two dedicated teams who have made all of this possible. John is a super team leader and has led many teams with us, to this vast Valley, for many years. For whatever it's worth, I salute you, John!

Our "Going Away Service" tonight was beyond anything I've ever seen or experienced. I was seated alongside the other Tuchauas that were present. Felt kinda powerful... Beginning with Pastor Joao, random villagers began bringing gifts to us calling for various members of the team, by name, to come and receive gifts.

All through the service, as I was attempting to either speak or interpret, several came up giving me rings and bracelets. I was moved and my heart broke. These Indians are caring people, but it is not characteristic for them to *"give"* anything away to anyone. Tonight, they freely gave of all they had. Finally, Tuchaua Joao thanked us, saying that he was grateful for the "physical things" that we did for his people, but he was *most* grateful for God's love that was expressed through us. He thanked us for sharing Jesus Christ with his people. That made the entire effort worthwhile to me.

Short list of gifts: Countless rings for me and group members; a number of necklaces for me; a number of bracelets for me and group members; a Satere Bible and hymnal for Pastor Judd; a canoe, paddle, and piece of thatch roof and siding from Tuchaua Joao to John.

It has been an unbelievably different trip, completely aside from the norm, if a "norm" even exists. God has revealed things to me. He has disciplined me. He has proven once again His faithfulness to me. I have indeed been humbled under His mighty hand. If I can only keep myself there...

Tuesday, July 31: What a great day to wake up to -- we're headed home! It's been a fantastic trip. The commander decided to stop on the top side of the *"sticks."* Too risky to continue on in the dark. Were underway at 5:30 A.M.

We stopped in Boa Vista do Ramos to take care of the workers and boat there. At the end of the next trip, we take the *Patrice* to be used on the Trombetas River. Gilberto desperately needs help on that river. He has so many new villages to be reached. I believe Patrice would be proud of the way her namesake's being used for God's Kingdom. No doubt she has already met (in heaven) a number of the fruits of this vessel's labors. Patrice was my cousin, taken in a car accident when she was only 18 years old. I remember having a crush on her. As I look back over time, most I've had a crush on or fallen in love with, haven't fared to well. Yep, for the sake of pretty much everyone out there, I'd best keep to myself...

> The thing that sticks out most in this entry are the affairs I continued to have and the effects they had on me and any hope of a normal, family life. I wasn't so concerned with Vic at the time. These separations were having profound effects on my children. They were growing and I felt they were becoming more aware of my dark actions. However devastating this all made me feel, I continued being the person that created it all. I would remember the faces of my children and have no other reaction but to cry and drink more...
> Alcohol in the veins of an alcoholic, will always wreak havoc on marriage and family. The baffling reality is, the alcoholic does not see it that way. There is always room for blaming the other party. Always the necessity to remain 'innocent' of all charges. All it takes is a drink to bring about acquittal. The jury in the alcoholic's mind has no choice but to absolve him for any and all wrongdoing. No harm done...

CHAPTER EIGHT

"If this is what life is about, I'll need relief and escape from it, every day. No doubt about it..."
**The 'haze' seems to be welcomed at this point.
I have no desire or inclination to change.**

A couple of weeks after 9/11, I'd moved my family back to Brazil until the dust settled from that tragedy. Just a few months later, I'd moved them back to the USA for another year, while I worked on solidifying the Trip Division of my organization. Vic and I seemed terminally separated by this time. But, its odd to say, were still hopeful for the restoration of our marriage at some point down the line. We still planned our home purchases, etc., together and she was taking more and more control of the finances because I was becoming more and more disinterested in such things.
I continued my "bitter" pleadings before God about alcohol. It seems I can do nothing to stop it. I am, more and more, expressing my shame through arrogance and the misuse of my power and position.

> *This exploratory trip is 'overtly' to spy out new*
> *waters where our teams might work. 'Covertly',*
> *it is for me to hire more key personnel so that*
> *I could further isolate myself from day-to-*
> *day activities and the public, in general.*
> *My drinking is particularly unbridled at this time*
> *and I don't want to stop. Can't imagine life without it.*
> *I need to make drinking possible, no matter what.*

EXPLORATORY TRIP TO THE ALTAIZ RIVER
March 13-18, 2002

Thursday – March 14
Don't think I've ever flown this much at one time. Arrived Sao Paulo yesterday morning. Then, connected here, to Manaus. I had a few hours before my flight to Santarem. So, I went and checked on a few aluminum hulls, for a friend of mine back in Dallas. I found the ones he thinks he might want. I'm having Serafin (our commander) go check it them out while I'm here today. The hulls are stored on the yacht next door to my boat. Nobody around to allow us onboard when I went. Maybe take a look at the later.

Arrived Santarem at 10:30 this evening. Checked in to the old Tropical Hotel, which is now owned by the Governor of Amazonas. What an honest man he must be. Came in to office 8 years ago without a pot to pee in. Must be a good steward of his salary to make an investment like this......I was so very tired when I finally laid down. The only bright spot, thus far, was a call around midnight from Vic's maid. Thank God this girl has agreed to keep me informed. All is well with the boys back home.

Vic is a piece of work right now. Moving out a couple of months ago was rough. Doesn't make any sense to me. I pay the bills. She lives like a Queen. Just can't leave well enough alone. Having to rent an extended-stay suite next door is causing a big strain on things. Don't understand why we can't be under the same roof and leave each other alone. The boys come over every day and every night. They spend more time with me than with her. I know it is confusing for them for me to be that close yet so far. What a mess...

Friday – March 15
The meeting this morning of the Paranorte Mission Board was a disaster. In anticipation of this inevitable result, I drank quite a bit last night. Had a tumbler-full when I woke up this morning as well and the coffee in my thermos was duly 'doctored'. I've *never* been so disappointed in this little group of men as I was today. Both mine and Earl's lawyers were present – might as well have been *two* lawyers for Earl! I missed Liza here today... The meeting ended up being a 'railroad job'. After about an hour, me and the two people that I had flown in to take over the mission, walked out. It was evident that Levando was running the show. He has become quite an accomplished little thief over the years, I'm afraid. What a jerk. And he has the audacity to call himself a "pastor"

It's just unfortunate that Alberto and Levando turned out this way. Alberto will regret his actions as President, for a long time to come. My relationship to him just took a nose-dive. But, I would never do anything to degrade or jeopardize the future of he or his family in any way.

I believe that a man is fully capable of making unwise decisions that ultimately compromise him in the eyes of his peers. I also believe that a man's past performance should weigh even more heavily in the equation. In life, a man only has one past. His future is undeterminable.

There are very dear people in my *own* life that have overlooked my pitfalls and shortcomings and support me today, as never before. The "demons" of one's actions are usually punishment enough for anyone. These "demons" don't rest – thus, the due sentence is laid down and carried out on its own. Doesn't need anybody's, outside help. I'd much rather be beat-up *really* bad, all at once, and be done with it. Rarely works that way though. Lord knows I'll be paying for *my* stuff for the rest of my life. Just hoping it's a short one...God bless you and keep you, Alberto and Levando. I continue to love you.

My brother was in town to meet me after the meeting. At the last minute, Dad asked me to take him along with me on this Altaiz exploratory. So, I agreed. We flew back to Manaus at 2:00 this afternoon.

Arrived in Manaus and were aboard the *Laura* at 6:00 PM. She was ready and waiting at the hotel port. Zeek is great. He got everything ready and waiting with a few phone calls from Minas. Don't *ever* want to lose him.

It's good to see him. Literally, a transformed man. God has done a mighty work in his life over the past couple of months. I'm proud of him *and* for him. He's thinking more clearly now. Has a better grasp of his life and future than I've seen in a while. God has a great work for him yet to do, I'm sure. We've had our serious differences over the years. I'm looking forward to something lighter this time around. After taking on some extra beer to tide us over, we set sail. Destination: Altaiz River.

Wellington (my driver) forgot the Sat-phone. We had to sail though. Could wait while he went after it. Put a tender-boat in the water and sent him after it. He finally caught up with us at 11:00

PM. He had a rough ride catching us. I think he will probably make up a better "final checklist", next time around...

Saturday – March 16
Man, we stayed up most of the night. We sat and drank until nothing we said, made any sense. Had a good time reminiscing about the past and waxing about the future.

My brother got married again. It's already going down the drain, it seems. This will be the fourth house and family he's gone through. At least the women are all well taken care of. Man, I wish he'd just stop getting married...

We hashed out a new "working arrangement" that may allow me to support him without having to relate to him as a "boss". Maybe let us to just be brothers. I'll create a "field coordinator" position, give him a boat and let him do as he pleases. Maybe it will work out for both of us this way. He can keep a finger on the pulse of things; I can concentrate of the bigger picture for a while. We'll see...

I awoke at 5:00 this morning. Feeling hazy and unwell. Took a few minutes to get a beer down without throwing up so I could safely have another. We were anchored inside a lake a few hours up the Altaiz. Bad storm as we traveled last night. The crew got hopelessly lost. So, here we are, somewhere on the water in the middle of the Amazon Valley. Man, this is great. I live for these moments. Uncertainty beats the hell out of predictability. Looking forward to whatever God has in store for the day.

I've asked God to show us 3-4 villages in need of His witness during this trip. I know He will provide abundantly. I'm just humbled that He has allowed me this privileged. I tell everyone that I know that I consider myself to be one of the most fortunate men on the face of this big earth. It is at times like these that I realize, all over again, that this is true. I am indeed, privileged…

The Altaiz River isn't as large (wide) as it looks on the map. It is actually a series of canals and lake systems – easy to get lost. We have no guide with us. I planned it that way. Don't want the help when I'm by myself. After all, this is an "exploratory trip". Let's just explore…

After no less than 6 stops to ask directions, we found what we were looking for. The village is called Mangeirinha (small mango tree), situated on lake Novo Mastro (New Mast). Really fine people here. Strictly Catholic. No evangelical presence. The only group that has ever come to minister to them is the Jehovah's Witnesses. Oh well, now that they have had a taste of camouflaged hell, we may just be able to show them Paradise…

I went up and met the President of the community. His name is Waldir. Also met the second in command, Aginaldo, and the sec. of edu., Jose Antonio. They have a huge school here and a brand-new community center.

I explained exactly what we wished to do here and why (talk about Christ). They agreed and accepted – Thank God.

The area this village serves is approximately 1,200 in population. The school alone has 600 students. This will be a great place to begin Kentucky's year with us. Even though 2-3 days here will not be enough to tend to everyone, it will be a good beginning. Has to be enough.

Talked with Vic this afternoon. Bless her heart. William had a skateboard accident yesterday. Broke two (not just one) fingers! Bless his heart!!!

Spoke with him for a minute to see how he was feeling. He said he was fine – especially when he got home and discovered the splint wouldn't interfere with his video games. What a trooper...

Phillip and Matthew sounded good as well. Little Matthews still doesn't know quite what to think about me being here on the Amazon. He's never seen it – doesn't understand – worries about my safety. It's touching that he thinks about me while I'm out here. I look forward to the summer when he (and the older boys) is here. What precious children. I love them so much. Without so much as a word, a world of Matthew's questions and concerns will be put to rest. Maybe Vic will reconsider and come, too. That might be the answer to a lot going on right now. It would also be the first time our family would be together in this big Valley. What an answer to prayer that would be.

I left the Sat-phone turned on after talking to Vic. My poor brother was sitting at the table where the phone sets. A very strange noise began sounding. After about 6 "gurgles", he realized it was the phone. He had never heard it ring before. He literally jumped back from the table like some beast was lunging at him! Had no idea what it was!! Oh well. It was dad on the line. Filled him in on the events of the day. Good to hear from him. Gonna have to check my brother's meds, I guess. His reaction to the phone was priceless, almost unworldly. If he's holding out on me about him having some hallucinogens, I'll be a little upset... (ha-ha)

It's 8:00 PM right now. The crew is worn out. Haven't rested at all in the last 24 hours. I had them anchor at 4 this afternoon just above the city of Altazes. I felt we had done enough for this day. Tomorrow we explore deeper south, up the Altaiz. Two more villages to find. "Finding" villages is not the problem – they are everywhere. I just want God to show me His villages. A grand work is about to begin here on the Altaiz River. I am grateful He is allowing me to be a part of it all...

Sunday – March 17

My brother and I decided to leave the beers alone last night. We are down to 4 cases and have another day ahead of us until we can pick up more. Slept well, and all night.

After "cruising" around for a couple of hours, we came upon a beautiful lake – Lake Tumbira. Most of the waters of the lakes we've seen, thus far, are not fully "black" water, yet. The water levels are rapidly rising now and the brown, Altaiz River waters are still encroaching on the lakes. Still, we've had no mosquitoes at all. It's been nice. The only unwanted visitors we've had are the "Poto". They seem to be fairly standard out here this time of year. This is a "peeing" bug that pees on you when it gets cramped in clothing and the likes. Its urine is like an acid. It doesn't hurt at all. Just leaves a burn wherever it touches you. Oh well, no such thing as a perfect world, huh?

Stopped at a house and visited for a while. Come to find out, the owner's wife is the "boss" of the community. So, we headed out in search for her. Finally found her way up in one of the headwaters. She'd been trying to herd up her runaway pigs to them home. Maybe I need a wife like that... Seems the "mama" pig keeps running away from home and all the others follow her off into the woods. So, the lady, Noemi, fixed the situation. She hunted the old mama pig down and butchered her on the spot – she thinks all the other pigs will stay home now. I think, if I were her husband, I'd try drawing a lesson from all this – I know there's **bound** to be one in this situation, somewhere. Maybe "there's no place like home..."? or, "better to live with a grumpy woman than......"?

The people of Tumbira are simple and kind. They are very receptive to our coming. This will be the second, and maybe final, village Kentucky will have the time to minister to. The total population is between 500-700. There is no "village" here. Just lots and lots of scattered houses. It reminds me a lot of the Trombetas region – Carimum, Salgado and Batata. We'll use the school and a cool looking "straw-hat", shaped structure for VBS. Medical will be at the little school house.

What we have tried to do on this trip is divide the river in three sections – Upper, lower and middle. I've drawn a map in what little of a mind I have left. We should, from these three points, be able to reach a **great** number of lakes over the coming years

God has a plan, I'm sure. We will carry it out as we follow His leadership and move along at His pace.

Stopped off at Altazes (the city) to top off fuel and provisions. Found enough beer to finish out the trip as well. Thank God. There was absolutely *no* fish for sale! All of it goes to Manaus – catches a much better price there. They *did* have beer. Lots and lots of beer. Priorities...

We've anchored in the "middle" region right now – how beautiful...Have our final village to check out tomorrow.

As for now, we have a little contest going on. A fishing tournament, so to speak. I've offered a bounty of R$ 10.00 for the biggest fish caught by the crew. The rules are simple: #1 - The guys have to fish from the *Laura*. #2 – Dinho (the cook) has to fish from the bow of the boat with everyone else, not from the kitchen area. We all figure he'd end up with an unfair 'bait situation' and that by morning, we'd have no more food onboard. He will have tossed it all off the stern to attract all the fish to his end...

Going to lay down early tonight. Won't try calling home. I know all is well. Vic and the boys are probably in San Antonio for the weekend at Sea World. We are, within reason, trying to make the best of these last couple of months in Texas. I've taken the boys to the Dallas Zoo, etc. It's been lots of fun. Just think it will be a long time before the boys see the USA again, after I move them back to Minas in May.

I'm looking forward to getting them settled in Brazil again. Vic and I committed to one year in the US to get the Trips Division on healthier ground and for the boys to get reacquainted with the language and culture. Their language is now about perfect – They are all A/B students. Unfortunately, the culture is going to take some time to rid from their minds.

The boys have been confused by the violence, perversion and prejudices in America. I have decided that, given the choice, I no longer wish to raise my boys in that environment. I love that country. But, I realize that I was raised in a different era. Things are different now – very different...Vic and I have been saving every dime we can over the past 6 months in order to buy a new house in Minas. It will take a couple more years – but we will get there.

Even with the great computer communications, internet, etc, that we have right now; I know I will be here in the US several months each year keeping things in-line. I'm just at the point that I would rather be away from my family with *them in Brasil* than in the USA for now. Doesn't feel good at all...

Monday – March 18
Got up at 4:30 this morning. Waited till sunrise and went ashore to the village of Sao Jose. Visited awhile with the homefolks. The leaders were in town for some sort of meeting. Come to find out this lake community has an Assembly of God and a Seventh Day Adventist presence. No need to waste *our* time and *God's* resources duplicating efforts and adding to the confusion. I'll be happy to care for them physically, but nothing more. So, we're head for home.

Uneventful cruise to Manaus. Took exactly 13 hours. Not bad at all. The *Laura* runs a little bit faster than the *Belatis*. I told dad we'd take care of this little, embarrassing problem. I'll just have a smaller prop put on the *Laura* – Like to see her catch us then. Being the "boss" *does* have its unfair advantages,,,

Arrived Manaus at 7:00 this evening. Lots to do before my flight to Minas. Met with several people about finishing our "floating house", repairs to the *Belatis*, etc. A Very productive time.

I'm now sitting at the airport in Manaus. It's 1:15 AM. My flight leaves in an hour.

This has been a great experience for me. I've been reminded of the weakness of the flesh from the meeting in Santarem. Evil *will* get its way when *greed* and *deceit* is permitted to be entertained, for even a glitch in time, in the human mind. The most stable of Christians *will* fall by their hand.

I've learned that it is important to forgive the wrongs that we see in others. Situations arise in life that tends to jade the absolutes that normally hold us firm and strong. When this happens, people must live with the consequences. However, we should *never* abandon or cease to help and support these people in the future. We never know when *our own* "I'd never do that..." might come home to haunt us in word, deed or thought.

I've been, once again, privileged to see and feel the hand of God working before my very eyes. The Spirit was there, ahead of me, every step of the way. He had already opened the doors and lightened the hearts of all whom I met along the Altaiz River. Kentucky's entry into this area will be smooth as silk. How beautiful it was to watch it all happen. Thank you Lord for allowing me to watch You work, first hand.

I have a peace in my heart and soul about my family. I'd like to think the right road is being followed. I just don't know how to walk it. I realize I may be the most glaring, broken cog in this wheel. I do fine for a time, then, I'm off again. God, help me with this. I have no idea how to change. I have not the strength to even think about change, much less act upon it. If anything good is to come of my life, You need to make that happen. If not, the only good that may come, will be in the ending of it. Do whichever is best. I don't really care at this point.

> I've dealt with what was needed to secure a bit of
> insulation from my duties. Although I am angered
> by those in my employee who had betrayed me,
> I feel smug inside – actually glad to be out from
> under the added responsibility, while being
> able to culpate someone other than myself.
> I've also taken on the care of my brother again.
> His duties will place a needed barrier between
> me and the field, allowing me to concentrate
> on the teams and their activities.
> The true nature of this move is to free up more
> 'personal' time while I am in the Amazon. My brother's
> presence, added responsibilities in purchasing
> for Wellington and Zeek's general management
> would allow me to sit, drink and make decisions
> without needing to be involved in the details.
> When I finished this Diary entry, I remember
> having just a 'couple' of drinks. I don't remember
> boarding the plane. I know I must have continued
> drinking during the flight to Sao Paulo because I slept
> through the 'final call' for my connection to Miami.
> I somehow arrived home two days later with no
> recollection of, or reasonable excuse for, the delay...

CHAPTER NINE

"Pray, work and drink. Then, drink while I pray and work. Next step: just drink – because. working and praying don't get the 'job' done..."

Well, sometimes things just speak for themselves. The wheels are beginning to loosen on my 'little wagon'. I'm more perplexed than ever about the alcohol. But, even as my attitude and behavior becomes more outrageous, I still believe it's just a matter of learning how to drink – not fully stopping. When I came across this particular Diary, I remembered it clearly, with 'fear and trembling'. How far down I have gone. Yet, it's nowhere near the depths that would soon follow...

FEBRUARY EXPLORATORY
February 14th - March 05th, 2003

Friday, 14th
The day started, on schedule, at 5:50 AM. Got the boys and Vic up to have breakfast before school. It is a good thing to have this

discipline for the family – left to themselves; they would all be getting up around noon and be happy...

Today is Vic and my 15th anniversary We began dating on February 14th, 1988 – were married in December of the same year. Happy Anniversary my Love...

I had our driver pick me up and take me to the airport at 9:00 this morning. It promised to be a *very* long day. ETA, Manaus – midnight...

I'm here at the Belo Horizonte airport, awaiting my flight for Brasilia/Manaus – Departs at 5:30 PM.

A little time for reflection...

Much has taken place in my life over the past several months. Vic was accepted to law school and began studies several weeks ago. She likes the material and, for sure, has the ability to talk and talk. She will be a very fine lawyer someday – wouldn't want her prosecuting me, for sure.

The boys have gone back to the rhythm of school and are enjoying having their days filled with activities once again. The holidays are terrible for all of us. Too much free time to burn, doing absolutely nothing. I think Vic and I are finally over the whole "Business Man of the Year" and "Lion's Club Benefactor of the Year", fiascos. I was so drunk at *both* the events I couldn't even stand to receive the honors. I tried to anyway. Thus, the fiascos...

It's a good feeling to be getting my hands in the "mud" once again. I deal with the Amazon, Organization, asset movements and maintenance, etc., every day from Minas. However, there is nothing quite like being on location feeling, smelling and tasting the work first-hand. I'm back in the saddle!

We are doing a good bit of mechanical work on the *Belatis* this year. New generators; new fuel pump, emergency bilge, A/C, starter, alternator, etc., etc....

Last year, we concentrated on the comfort of the volunteers. This year, we are caring for the items with 10 years + usage. We are literally replacing *all* of the equipment that *has* or *will* falter in the mainframe and electrical systems of our vessel. Our new generators are three times the size of the ones being replaced. The new ones are 52hp/30kw. What a relief it is to have more power than we need instead of pushing our equipment to the limit, 24/7...

We are also ventilating the kitchen – It has been a hot spot for sure. Also on the agenda is a vapor-cooling system for the hammock areas upstairs. Not sure if, and how, it will work, but we are going for broke. The trip back up-stream for the groups is very hot – wind at our backs for up to 50 hours. We will do our best to compensate.

God has been very good to provide in the past months of no income for salaries, etc. I have, on purpose, not sought to know what our bank statement has looked like – I can't help the situation. Through a couple of close friends, we have made it through the "dark hours". Thank you – you know who you are...

Back to the here-and-now; I'll be on my boat tonight around midnight. I look forward to walking over the decks and inspecting it for hours. Thank God I arrive in the middle of the night – That way, I have her all to myself. By my estimates now, I probably won't hit my bed until 4 AM. I'll enjoy the "private, unguided tour" very much though.

I entrust, as always, my family to God's good care. I'll be gone for several weeks – He will care for them better than I – He always does; always has...

Saturday, 15th

Well, I arrived here on the *Belatis* at 2:00 AM. When we left Brasilia, had to return because a wing (or something) was about to fall off the plane. Anyway, they got the wing put back on and we proceeded with a delay of roughly 2 hours.

Upon arrival, the *Belatis* looked fantastic. The hold is open due to generator installation, etc. None the less she is beautiful. Denilson met me with a cold beer as I was coming up the ramp. This guy is worth *every* penny I pay him...

The crew were still up, cleaning the *Laura* for my trip. She looks good, shining in the dark. Later today, the crew will change out the prop and do some final touch-ups. She'll be ready to sail by nightfall.

I called home this morning. Last night was the party for Matthew's 9th birthday. Everybody was sleeping in. Talked to the maid – at least all are well. Glad I missed that one, too. Remembering what I remember of William's last party, I made a mess of things. He was so happy I was there for a change. I've missed too many over the years. To be fair, I've even missed the ones I attended...

This last one, Vic tells me I was the only one stumbling around, making a fool of myself. I ended up under the waterfall of the pool, trying to get our dogs to join me. All this, before 8 PM. At least most of his little friends hadn't arrived yet. How utterly embarrassing for him. Don't know *what* happens that *that* happens. Can't remember any of it for the life of me...

I decided to double our fuel capacity on the *Laura*. We will install an extra 2000 liters worth. This way, we won't have to re-fuel "on the road". The fuel we acquire here in Manaus is more dependable, clean. By increasing our capacity, we will be able to do our trips without depending on "interior" fuel. Good deal.

The Laura

It's noon and Zeek is out taking care of business. I have a meeting here on the *Belatis* set for 2 PM with potential crew for my trip with John and Jack. Everybody wants pay increases – I'll do what I can...

Sunday, 16th
My brother came out today for a visit. It was good to see him again – he looks and sounds great! We talked about the trips, the organization and family. Had a great several hours together. I refused to drink with him. Last time we did, Denilson had to jump in to keep us from literally cutting each other. We set up a rule that no knives would be allowed when there was alcohol involved in the mix. How stupid...

The rest of the day was spent on details with Zeek. Still *much* work to be done.

Matthew's birthday party was yesterday evening. Didn't have a good cell signal or any way to get to shore to a line phone to call him – I'm sure he had a good time.

I'm looking forward to this trip – getting underway. Tomorrow will be a full and hectic day. It is now 7:00 pm. Almost time to lie down. It's been dark for an hour and I'm tired.

Finally got a hold of Vic and Matthew – I'll sleep better now. It's strange. I hesitate to have a beer before I hear from home. I've got this fear that if I do, something bad will happen. I don't care how silly that sounds. Just true...

Sitting here alone, finally. "Alone". What a concept. It's not just a descriptive word for me. It is how I feel, even when there's people around. I've always claimed that I'm "my own best company". When I really ponder this, I see it to be true. If I am to feel alone, I should just be that way. But, it scares me. This is all a bit confusing. I like to drink. Almost need to sometimes. It keeps people away from me. At the same time, I want people to be around, just not bothering me. What a dichotomy of feeling.

At any rate, here I sit with 2 cases of beer in the cooler. Don't plan on leaving any "survivors" by sunrise...

Monday, 17th
Long hard day – promises to be a rough one for us all. The day before departure is always taxing. I'm feeling like crap, as usual. Forced down 2 beers already. Waiting to feel right again before getting started.

Dad's new 30 hp Honda engine arrived to be installed at 11:00 this morning. Took a lot of "adapting". Took *all* day – going to have to work out the kinks on the road. Didn't like pulling my guys off their jobs for such a thing. But, I love my Dad. What can I say...

Zeek didn't get started on the final fueling and purchasing until 8 this evening. Good thing there is not a lot left to purchase and the "big" stuff (water, etc.) was all boarded yesterday. He does a great job of things.

The "Commander Vasquez" is docked beside us. It lives next door. I inspected it again this afternoon. What a vessel to buy for our trips. The owner needs to sell it badly. The engine is a Scania. Just needs generators, etc. I guess I can dream...

Tuesday, 18th
The flight arrived on time. Big surprise for me! The first ones out the door of customs were Hyde, Jackson. and several others from so many years back. Didn't have very much time to visit, but it was good to see them, none the less. These guys saved my life back in '97. I was really strung out during a business trip Dallas. Seemed like the end of the road. They got me into a treatment center for a few months. Didn't think I needed it, but it helped dry me out. The mission organization I helped found for them is doing well. Glad I'm not involved with it any more. Just different philosophies and goals. I wish them well.

Me and the "J's" were underway by 4 this morning. Jack and I started on some cold ones the second we got aboard. SO good to "sip" with him again. Been awhile...

Everything went well until about midway down the Parana da Eva. Had a stress fracture in the prop – One of the blades simply dropped off. Unlike the *Belatis*, we were cruising again within an hour or so.

The *Belatis*'s 46" brass mass, would have taken a wench and half-a-day to change out...

Everyone just slept on and off all day. ETA, Maues is set for 10:00 pm.

I've been looking forward to this exploratory trip. Plan on seeing several new places along the Maues and Andira Rivers. God will be faithful in showing us where to bring Florida's two groups this summer. Lord, teach and show me what You would have me to learn. Fill my cup Lord. It is so very empty right now. Help me slow down on the drinking. Don't feel like drinking. Just don't feel well enough *not* to drink. Fix this, please...

Wednesday, 19th
Woke up around 4 this morning. Got Pr. Jose onboard and were headed upriver by 7:30.

Stopped at Esperanca, picked up Tuchaua Evaristo to accompany us in to the Satere Nation. We are alone this trip – no work planned, etc. So, Jose felt we should be accompanied by a chief as we travel and visit.

Man, what a trip this is turning into. Just "busted up" another prop! One per day is going to get really old, *very* quickly!!! The channel here on the Marau River side is very tight and curvy. I've never been here when the water is low – Big difference.

Had the johnboats in the water the entire day helping turn the *Laura* through the twists and turns. Lost count of how many turns were too tight to make unattended. And we're supposed to bring the *Belatis* up here in July. She's 3 *times* the size of the *Laura*...

Got within 15 minutes of Vila Nazare at 6:30 pm – too dark to continue. This creek is running so fast up here, near the headwaters. It's going to be a "thrill" heading back down tomorrow....

Going to have to switch to vodka, I guess. Got too many "preaches" and "chiefs on the boat to risk beer-breath. Vodka does the trick. Just makes for a heavy "day after". Need to moderate a bit.

Thursday, 20th
What a day this has been. Got up on schedule and ventured in to Nazare just after dawn. I was here last year for a brief visit during one of my earlier trips. The people up this far are different. They seem to respect the opinions and advice of the Elders of the community. We sat around and drank Sapo and visited for a couple of

hours. Have *no* idea what was being said! Just sat there and drank Sapo, listened and nodded my head when it seemed I was expected to. Tried something else new while I sat there – the Satere equivalent of Tacaca. My goodness, I have *never* tasted anything so "pepper" hot in my life! It is made up of tapioca "goo", tucupi (form the manioc root) and, finally, just about every hot pepper they could find this side of Venezuela!! Know what though? I *loved* it...

Well, after the formalities, we walked around and did some measuring for a possible water system. Made no promises as we departed. Promises go *along* way with these people. Much caution must be used in the words we use. They have had so many people promise them things and then bail...

Started our "cruise" down-creek at 10:30 am. What a ride! We were directed by the johnboats. The *Laura* was pretty much in reverse gear the whole way, just trying to compensate for the strong current. About an hour into the ride, we went through a "short-cut" and ran aground. Now, mind you, when you run aground going up-stream – it's not real, big deal. However, when you make this mistake headed *down-stream*, in a swift current, it becomes a much *bigger* deal...

Cako and Jose were pulling and pushing from the stern and bow of the *Laura* while Serafin was in the water rocking the boat and I was manning the wheel in reverse gear. Well, with all this effort, we finally backed off the sandbar 45 minutes later. With the *Be*, we might have been there until around May! I stayed at the wheel till we reached our next stop, Nova Aldeia.

As the day progressed, we were able to stop, meet and visit the Tuchauas of all the villages on this remote river. Mauricio of Nazare; Clementino of Nova Aldeia and Cazusa of Boas Novas. We stopped, both coming and going, at Vila Nova to visit the Grand Tuchaua. Both times, he was gone. I guess the important thing is that we tried...

Dropped Evaristo off at Esperanca by dark and headed down stream to Maues. Called and spoke with Vic and the boys – how sweet is to hear their voices – all is well...

Friday, 21st
Woke up at the usual 4:00 am. Didn't drink at all last night. Told myself I wouldn't, and I didn't. Kinda proud of myself. Come to find out that Jose got us lost last night. I woke up at around 10 last night – I could since a storm brewing to the East. When I got to the pilothouse, I found that we were only an hour out of Esperanca, *again.* Jose had gotten us turned around *so badly* that we were still 5 hours from Maues – I gave him a new name. He will now be known as "Moses" for his "wanderings" in this liquid wilderness...

It is now 8 in the morning. John and Jack are out roaming the town. Serafin and Cako just left to take the shaft-flange of our main engine to be welded (this universal joint was repaired in Manaus just a couple of days ago – here we go again...). They also took the generator exhaust and our two props for repairs. I figure the prudent thing to do is get the repairs done *here* where the right professionals and equipment are available. We have a long way to go on this trip. Best to be prepared.

Jose came to me with documents for me to sign donating the *Burtis* to him. I re-considered doing so. I assume the presidency of our Brasilian affiliate in just a few days. All equipment will be donated to that entity – from there, we will decide as a group what to do with things. For me to start moving assets now, might complicate the integrity of my assuming the directorate.

You know, I haven't been feeling very well these past few days. I have felt nausea and a constant little pain in my right side. I've limited my food intake to soup, twice per day. Reduced fluids to water and very little coffee for today. I know the alcohol has a little to do with it. But, this isn't just a hangover. I'll see how it progresses. I have just prayed that I feel better for my meetings as the trip develops – I know He will provide.

You know, being away from and boys has become a more difficult task over the past several years. I have always been told, "it becomes easier" over time – it has not. Quite the contrary. As my boys grow up and my love increases for them, this distancing from them becomes more heart wrenching – more intense. This too I have placed before the Lord. I trust that these precious gifts will be by my side, out here, more and more. I have also prayed that Vic's fear of flying will subside. She doesn't come with me because she dreads the "getting here" too much. God is almighty. He can change anything He desires.

My drinking is also of great concern to us all. Hard as I try, I can't seem to fully control it once I start. Bigger problem yet is, I can't seem to control *when* I start as well as I used to. My memory of what happens when I drink is also becoming "iffier". I don't think I do and say *near* what Vic says I do when I drink. I feel she may be trying to manipulate me with it. Regardless, I need to figure out a better way or just stop. God, help me, please…

The boys just got one of the props put back on the *Laura*. Still waiting for the U-joint flange and exhaust. I just want to get underway…

It's 2:00 pm. Still dead in the water. The "new" flange snapped as we backed out – what a thrill…

So, here we sit. I went ahead and gave the order to eliminate the U-joint completely and hook the shaft directly to the reduction gear. Simultaneously, sent Cako to try and get a new flange tooled for us – I don't hold out much hope for that getting all this done. Not today, anyway. Cako brought me two more bottles, each, of scotch and vodka. Really wish he hadn't done that. But, what the hell...

I was able to call Zeek in Manaus. He was beside himself. He went down to the Captain of the Ports to begin getting the documentation in order for the *Belatis's* trips. Found out *all* the rules have changed. We are having to start from scratch. New boat floor plan and classification or no travel. When it rains it pours...

I got him calmed down and asked him for the 1-2-3, step-by-step, of what needed to be done. At least that got him to slow down his thinking and rationalize more clearly. He will start the paperwork today – will probably take him another two weeks in Manaus to get it done.

You know, I'm just glad all of this is happening *now* instead of June 1st when the Kentucky team is about to get here. No such thing as a smooth trip, but we wouldn't need *this* kind of "mountain to climb" at *that* point.

God is truly in control. We are going to carry on with this trip, as planned. If we deem it necessary and prudent to discontinue, God will call that shot – we will follow. As for now, everything is being taken in stride. John actually said that he was glad to see some of the negative little things that usually go on behind the scenes – Makes him more comfortable now when we lose a prop with a group, etc. I'm just glad he never noticed these things during a group trip. That means *we* are doing *our* job...

Don't think I will call Vic today. I've already had a bit to drink. Not a lot of "good news" to share, anyway. I know she is fine there, and we are too, here.

2:40 PM – Looks like the flange is getting made after all. I sent Serafin up to overlook the situation. Supposed to be ready by 4:00. Either way, we've done all we can and are ready to travel either way the coupling is made between the engine and shaft. At this point, I will probably have the boys take us a couple hours out of Maues, after fueling, just to be able to say we made some "forward" movement today... The crew is tired – been diving without gear, all day long. They deserve a good night of rest and sleep...

Well, so much for a tranquil afternoon. It's 4:15 pm now. We are here in port, without power, going through one of the worst wind and rain storms I've had the pleasure of experiencing. The Maues Bay is famous for these. Normally though, we have power to ride it out. This time, we are dead in the water. Several mid-size boats were ripped from their mooring and floated off. Cako went out in one of our Jon's and retrieved a couple of them. We are well tied off with lateral lines. Still, the wind is abnormally gusty. Oh well – this is what the Amazon Valley is all about. You prepare for her and then, respect her when she does things you don't expect her to...

4:30 PM: Serafin just returned with the new part. He is installing it as I write. Lord, let it be as you wish. However, my desire is that it works, and we can pull away from here.

It is 8:00 PM. It looks like the flange is holding up. It has been a *very* long day for the crew and me. We backed away from Maues, fueled and anchored in a safe-harbor around the bend. Going to let the crew sleep until the full moon appears (probably around

2:00 AM). Then, we will get underway. I'm exhausted but am finally enjoying a stiff drink. The day is done.

Saturday, 22nd
Underway for Boa Vista do Ramos at 4:00 this morning. The *Laura* is still running well for us – Thank God

Arrived in Boa Vista at 8:00. The Bible Institute was scheduled to begin here this morning but, Raimundinho hasn't arrived yet. So, we visited the church and Pr. Gildo for a little bit and decided to head on down to meet Raimundinho on his way up-river. It is imperative that I speak with him about the Andira River area. He is apparently bringing all the laborers from the Satere's with him to the institute. That may present a problem with our entering the Nation on our own. We'll find that out in a couple of hours I guess.

I didn't sleep very well last night. Dreamed some "weird" stuff. The most shocking one was that I returned home to find Vic had become a wealthy woman. When I asked how she did it, she told me that she had traded me for a wealthy man... Well, I guess that would be a way she'd do it...

Anyway, just talked to Dad and Mom. Good to hear their voices. They got back last night – been traveling in the USA as long as I have in the Amazon this week. Took care of a little business – wish he could be here with me to have some quality time together. Someday soon, I hope. This is a crazy family we have. We seem to pass each other in the night. We each take care of our different work, making it a challenge to be in the same place at the same time. However, we are always together through a common cause, prayer and Spirit...

Met up with the "*Jesus Me Ama*" (Raimundinho's boat) at about 11 this morning. Was good to see him. This little man is only small in stature – in faith, he is second to very few that I know. I was humbled as his boat came alongside the *Laura* in the middle of the river for our rendezvous. There were at least 25 lay pastors hitching a ride to the RBBI. I many times complain at having a single extra person onboard – pitiful...

Had a good visit as we floated downstream. We got all the information we need to enter the Andira Satere Nation. We had prayer together and parted ways. I look forward to venturing into unknown waters – Man, I live for this!

Passed by Barreirinha at 1:15 pm. Dropped off a "hitch-hiker" we picked up in Boa Vista. We didn't dock though – just sent the Jon boat in.

We are now cruising toward the mouth of the Andira River, just above Parintins. Should be there by dark. We will try to make it up to Freguezia before stopping for the night – all depends on the wind. The Bay of the Andira is almost as violent as the Maues. If the wind is up, we will seek safe-harbor for the night, just inside the mouth.

Spoke with Zeek earlier. It looks like we may be able to get away without reclassifying the *Belatis* if I can get it donated to our affiliate. Great news! Problem is, it places urgency for me to get to Oriximina, ASAP. The conflict here is that we came to visit the Andira River – this we will do. I just trust the Lord will allow us good weather and speed to get it done so that I can be in Oriximina by Monday night – Lord, it's up to you...So much to do there.

Started reading in the Book of Acts today – fascinating. I read in Psalms and Proverbs daily. The Acts are going to be fun and enlightening.

It's 4:20 and we are already in sight of Freguesia – *way* ahead of schedule. I've had a bit to drink and don't feel like visiting with anyone. We decided to continue on upstream until dark, bypassing Freguesia until we return downstream.

Sunday, 23rd

Dropped anchor last light at 6:40. We are at the edge of the unknown – Ariau is off our starboard side. Straight ahead, the Satere Nation. It's 6:00 am and we just got underway.

Slept off and on last night. More dreams about Vic. The dreams are getting better and better though – won't go in to much detail...

I'm eager to see where God and this river has for us to today – what a *rush* to be going "where few white men has ever gone"...

It's 7:30 and the J's are out trolling for whatever they might catch. The banks of the river up here are beautiful and sandy. We are just idling up, as they play. By everybody's estimates, we are still about an hour from our stopping point, Ponta Alegre. This is where the FUNAI outpost is and where Raimundinho asked us to stop and visit.

Arrived Ponta Alegre at 8:20. Quite a large village. Went in and met the FUNAI agents, Flavio and Arthur, and explained who we were. Raimundinho had not been able to call ahead and announce we were coming After a half-hour of chitchat, we were welcomed with open arms.

First stop was to visit Tuchaua Mikilis. What a character! He is the oldest Tuchaua of the entire Satere Nation. Born in 1913 and is still ruling. Not bad...

We gave him a stick of guarana as a gift. When I told him we had gotten the stick from Tuchaua Evaristo over on the Maues side of the Nation, he just grinned and told us that Evaristo was his nephew – small world, huh.

Mikilis is passing his Reign to his son-in-law, Amado. Rightfully, this "passing" would have been to his own son. Well, his son was killed by bow-and-arrow in a dispute with another tribe some 20 years ago. Thank God, the days of those kinds of disputes are gone now. Hopefully...

We walked through the village as we visited. The primary needs on this side of the Satere's is medical. unlike the Maues side where the major need is water. So, our teams to the Andira will be heavy on the medical tilt.

Went across the river (Tuchaua wanted to go for a ride too, so he came along). Santa Fe is the name of the place. It is here that we will complete a church building for Raimundinho. There are few houses at this point, but the idea is to grow a new community. In Ponta Alegre, there are already an Assembly of God and 7th day Adventist churches. They are both dead but, no need to build on top of them. If their churches are dead, why put another one there just to add to the cemetery. I'm pretty much fed up with this whole church building thing. I was speaking with a colleague in the USA a while back. He was so excited about something called "church planting". He said that it had to do with establishing new churches where there weren't any. As the conversation continued, he mentioned a neighborhood in Florida that I happened to be familiar with, knowing it already had at least a couple of churches established there. When I asked him about it, he answered enthusiastically, "But, there's not a *Baptist* one there, yet." Well, of course. Silly me...

The Andira, Satere Nation is different than the Maues side in several ways. The needs are different; the typography is different; and the people are more "civilized". Also, there are 40 of the 56 villages on this side.

Maues side is definitely the most challenging, logistically. Any way you look at it though, they both need our help.

Departed at noon. Headed for a quick stop in Freguesia. Then on to Oriximina either tonight or early in the morning.

Arrived Freguesia at 3:30 this afternoon. We were only going to run up and say hello to the folks – were only going to stay 30 minutes. So much for that! Finally departed at 5:00 pm. Ended up visiting with Cilene and her new baby; Sabia had to squeeze us some fresh passion fruit juice and on and on... Got to see just about everybody though. I haven't been here in two years. All the children have grown so much. Several of the older folks our teams took care of for so many years have died off. A lot happens in two years. Lord, thank you for allowing me to stop here once again. Please provide a way that one of the groups to this area may stop re to these precious ones.

We are headed for Oriximina right now – ETA set for midnight. The J's and I are of one accord: We take care of business in Oriximina tomorrow. Then, tomorrow evening, we head straight for Aveiro. From there, back down and we all catch a plane to Manaus in time for them to catch their flight home. We'll see how it all fits together. Whatever it is, will be ok and according to God's timing.

Just talked with Vic for a minute. Told her of my plans over the next few days – everybody is well at home. Who knows, I may get down her way a couple of days early – that would be great. However, the work gets done *first* no matter how long it takes.

It's coming up on dusk right now. The sunset is going to be a good one. I'm going to ride out here on the bow until I get sleepy. Cako just brought out an ice bucket and glass for the "medicine" he picked up the other day in Maues. I knew I needed something for the pain in my side. Cako is a *fine* doctor a good doctor...

Thanks for the day Lord. It's been extremely full – I like that... Thanks again for the opportunity to be a part of Your work in the world. Don't deserve to be where I am. Seems I've done about everything in life *not* to be here. Don't know why You continue to shine on me. Really don't know...

It's 6:35 pm. Within the hour, we will be making the crossing of the mighty, main Amazon River at Parintins. It is always an experience. Hopefully, the winds will be down – the *Laura* is a sturdy vessel but "bounces" around considerably more than the *Belatis*. Like a Porsche in a cornfield... Anyway, I'll stay up through the crossing – shouldn't take more than a couple of hours. Have more than enough scotch to see us through. Then, it will be "hammock time"...

Monday, 24th
Well, so much for sleep last night. After crossing the Amazon, a violent wind and rainstorm hit us. *Unbelievable* gusts. We've been just inching along for hours. The river is full of floating debris (logs, etc.). At 2 this morning our spotlight burned out. Jack. had a portable one that allowed us to get to shore to replace it – it was pouring sheets of rain through the whole process. It is now 3:00 – still inching along. Either things get better real soon or I will have them pull over and dock till daybreak. Not a bad idea...

Arrived in Oriximina at 7:20 this morning. Not much sleep at all, and such a BIG day ahead. Feeling like crap...

Oriximina

Went up to Grace's with John and Jack and Pr. Gilbert. Met with Liza all morning. Then, about lunchtime, my brother just shows up, out of the blue! He was on his way to the airport, headed home to Manaus – great seeing him.

As I met with Liza, Herbert and Grace, contemplating the trip to the Hospital. I couldn't get a peace about all the storms we've been having on the Big River. The *Laura* is a bit small for some of the stuff I've been seeing, plus, all the mechanical problems she's been experiencing.

So, I decided to sign a limited power-of-attorney over to Liza to take care of the Hospital. If I were by myself, without the responsibility for the J's, I'd go ahead. As it is, we will head up-stream for Manaus at first sign of the moon tonight.

Had everything taken care of with the mission by 4:00 PM. We are waiting for the "new" flange to be made **again** – Third flange; Third town... We have done all we came to do – It's time to go home...

I have now reached the point where most alcoholics find themselves in the late-stages of the disease. I have resigned myself to the fact that 'this is the way I am and will probably always be.' 'God' and 'alcohol' are mentioned in the same breath. I talk to Him as if he were a 'drinking buddy'. It is a twisted relationship I've created to feel connected to Him in some way. My mind and heart are reconciled that 'drink' is a permanent fixture in life. God will have to live with me, just the way I am. Alcoholics are desperate for peace and serenity. Their drinking increases, exponentially, when they find these are not possible. They don't truly know why peace of mind eludes them. They blame circumstances, places and things, refusing to look inward. They somehow know their soul is dying but have become impotent to stop the digression. The feeling of 'Impending doom' is a constant. Only another drink can subside their loneliness and fear...

CHAPTER TEN

**"How dark it is just before the dawn..."
A loneliness was descending upon me. One that
only another alcoholic could recognize.**

*The following diary entries, a year apart,
record the beginning of a relationship that will
ultimately save my life and lead me to sobriety.
Mike is from Alabama. His story could fill volumes
on its own. God placed him in my path long
before I was able to realize 'why' he was there.
I would continue on my downward spiral for another
two years before making the pivotal call to Mike that,
by God's Grace, would lead me to where I am today.
The final paragraph of the 2004 entry,
frighteningly illustrates the rapidity with which
my resolves could evaporate. It made me shudder
when I read it again after all these years...*

BOYD WALKER

BETWEEN THE TRIPS IS ALWAYS A CHALLENGE
MANAUS, AMAZONAS
June 10, 2004

Between the trips is always a challenge. This time will be no different. Much to do. I feel totally alone. I miss my family and long to be in the security of their presence. I feel scared, even a bit paranoid. It's like something really horrible could engulf me at any moment. I'm lost. I'm done, but don't think I can stop what will necessarily come to pass...

I got the Alabama group safely into the Tropical Hotel several hours ago. Right now, I should be taking a nap, but sleep eludes me. I am scheduled to meet the team for dinner at 7 this evening. It will be a good diversion from the solitude.

As this team arrived through the Gate at the airport last week, Mike was the last one out. I met him last year. We talked a bit during the trip. I didn't get into specifics. Just told him I was having some difficulties. I somehow feel a kindred spirit between us. At the airport, he had looked at me and said, "when you're done, give me a call". Well, when we hugged as he left the boat this afternoon, a year later, he said the *very* same thing to me. Nothing more; nothing less. Still not sure exactly what he meant. But, I do feel done. He gave me his cell number. We'll see.

I called and spoke with Phillip this morning. I wished him a Happy Birthday. It is his 13th. I told him that he was now a man and that I would pray for him daily – this, I have done and will continue to do. Got to talk with William and Matthew too. All is well and all are getting along just fine. Vic is a bit under the weather. I pray she feels better soon. There is still such a long stretch of time away and I dare not contemplate how I miss them so...

I ask of You Lord, that You guard me, protect me and keep me focused on the work yet to be done. The season has just begun. I need strength and assurance from You, continuously. I need your presence manifested in my life *now*, more than ever before. I know that you will provide. I just wish that I knew how and when. I will do all that I can and then leave it to you. I ask you for good rest and good fellowship. I need your presence dear Lord...

It's time to start thinking about getting ready for dinner. I am really too tired to go but will do so anyway. I'm feeling the fatigue of the past 9 days. My mind isn't working very well. My body feels on the verge of collapse. I just want to rest. To be honest, I just want a few beers. I know it won't lead to much good. But, I really don't care at this point. Zeek said he's made sure the fridge in my cabin is stocked. Screw dinner. Zeek can get the team to the airport on his own. They can forgive my absence. I need to get feeling right. Think I'll turn my phone off and just sit on the deck for a while tonight.

ALABAMA PRE-TRIP
July 10th – 23rd, 2005

Sunday, July 10, 2005

I woke up at 3:30 this morning with a mind full of thoughts. In a few hours, my group of ladies will be gone, and I will be visiting with Dad and Mom at the hotel downtown. Later in the night, I should be picking up the boys and Marcos at the airport, but I called Vic earlier to cancel their trip down here. I'm in no shape to receive them. She knows I'm drunk. I don't really care anymore.

I have been sitting here drinking and thinking about the entire management picture, under Zeek. I don't like what I see. The mistreatment of the staff, not obeying my direct requests, lack of conclusive financial reporting, etc, etc... Last night was about the culmination of it all. Well, just forget it. I'm going to fire him.

The whole thing is going to come to a head over the next couple of days. In a way, I look forward to it – at least it will be done. I fully expect him to threaten to go home and I know that I will call his bluff and send him home. This will leave a temporary void in our system here but nothing that, after this double trip coming up, cannot be handled with surgical precision. I will hire Wellington to just do the purchases for the remaining three trips of the Season. The more I think about the absence of Zeek, the more I like it.

Running *no* simultaneous trips next year and running various trips on the *Laura* will eliminate the need for a "full-time" manager. I can handle all but the maintenance of the vessels through 3rd party contracting.

I am so very pissed off right now that I'd fire Zeek on the spot if he were here. I have a great distaste for him at this moment. He sent replacements for my crew at 11 PM last night. The replacements were "cutting their hair", etc. What a total lack of respect for hard working men. This will not go unaddressed.

It is 5:45 and the sunrise is blocked by the rain clouds. I just made the mistake of venting a little of my frustrations about Zeek, to Ronaldo and Cako. It'll probably come back and bite my ass. This happened when I simply asked them what they did on the *Belatis* while I was gone. The list they reeled off to me represented about 3 days of work and didn't include the primary things I ordered done – install a new water cooler and flushing the exhaust on the secondary generators.

It is 10:30 this morning – I just want to rest. I called Dad and cancelled my going to see him this afternoon. Just too tired. Just turned off my phone and opened a beer. Have a 1,000 more of them in the freezer. Finishing them off is all I want to do today.

Tomorrow we celebrate Mom and Dad's anniversary, here aboard the *Belatis*. Need to concentrate on *those* preparations for now.

Monday, July 11, 2005

Woke up in a freakin daze a few minutes ago. It's 5 AM. I'm shaking like a leaf. Feel like throwing up. What else is new. The chefs and other staff will be coming aboard in a bit. Hope I feel better by then.

All the guests were onboard the *Belatis* by Noon. Lunch was served. Good meal of Pirarucu, Tambaqui, chicken, etc, etc. Couldn't eat a thing. Had vodka in my coffee instead. I think everybody loved it. Among the guests were Eunice, Anna, Norton and his wife, Tommy and Tubby, Wellington and his family and a couple of others. I had not seen several of these people in years. Mom and Dad seemed to enjoy it.

I am concerned about Mom and Dad. Dad had an "episode" and was taken to the emergency room the day before they came down here. Mom is making herself sick worrying about Dad. I just wish they would move down to Minas where I could take care of them. There is no real way that I can move to the USA to take care of them there. My responsibilities are here. Lord, show me what to do about all of this and I will do it. In the meantime, continue to take care of Mom and Dad, ok?

Tuesday, July 12, 2005

Woke up on schedule this morning – 3:00 AM... Didn't have any beers before seeing mom and dad. Show a little respect, I guess.

I will go pick up Mom & Dad to have our portrait made – something Mom really wants done. I just want to be done with this visit entirely.

For the past several days I have had a dry cough. Well, it is now down in my chest and I feel a little feverish. I was going to start a "Z" Pack this morning, but they are not where I left them last week. Unfortunately, they have probably all been given away. I hate it when my action packers are meddled with while I am gone. I really don't know what to do with my attitude towards my management right now. I need to tone down and let some things slide, but it is getting increasingly harder to do so.

I really wish I could get a little more sleep between these trips. Just the thought that another 2 groups will be here and in full swing within 48 hours is tiring to me. I will try for some quality sleep during the trips. I don't drink as much when we have guests. Maybe slow down a bit. Actually looking forward to it...

I think what I am going to do is strongly consider, for next year, paying Wellington to do the purchasing and hiring for the year and see how it goes. He knows his way around and can figure the rest of it all out pretty quickly. I don't need a "trip manager" on the actual trips themselves. I mainly need a good purchasing agent and personnel director. Well, these are just thoughts about it all. We shall see. Lord, I still ask that You step in and take care of this deal. I just want to do it right and make everyone involved at least comfortable with the idea of eliminating Zeek's position.

My chest seems to be getting worse by the minute. I want Zeek to get his butt out of bed so he can tell me what he did with the "Z" packs. I need to start one ASAP.

Well, I am really tired again and it is almost time to "get up". I know it is a combination of this thing in my chest and fatigue. Got to get it together in the next 48 hours...

It is Noon right now. Pictures are taken and Mom and Dad are on their way to the airport. I had Wellington take them. I've had enough "visiting" to last me for a while.

Sitting here on my *Belatis*. I feel like crap about the way I've avoided the Parents during their brief stay. I know they just wanted to be near me. Been a long time. One day I'll probably regret my behavior. But, not now. A few beers will smooth all this out. No, a *whole bunch* of beers is what it's gonna take. No problem...

By the end of this 2005 entry, it is clear I've managed to seclude myself almost entirely. I was avoiding interaction with anyone, including my children and parents even though I loved them deeply. I knew my drinking was out of control. I knew it was affecting every relationship I had to family, staff and within the Organization. But, was unable to help myself at all. My resulting attitude towards life is negativity. The only emotion readily available to me is 'anger'. 'Oblivion' has become my only, true friend. He is as dependable as the air I breathed...

CHAPTER ELEVEN

*"I'll do it my way. It is the only way it will
work, until it no longer does…"*
*We are at a Bible Institute. I no longer believe we should
be 'preparing pastors' to engage in dogma. I am broken.
There is no way out. I am all but through questioning my
thoughts and actions. The end seems near, and I welcome it.*

As I re-read this log, for the first time after
having written it originally, I was taken aback
by how much I had degenerated in every
way a man could possibly degenerate.
I am defensive of my affairs with other women, as well
as the drinking. I have also developed a new-found
disrespect for my father. Although he knows about the
drinking, I had never before done so openly, with him
near me. This had changed and I made no apology for it.
The measures I used to take in order to hide my
alcoholism, are quickly disappearing from my
modus operandi. I am becoming careless and
unconcerned about hiding anything, anymore.
Reading my thoughts and reliving this complex
experience of juggling the spiritual and the flesh,

> *I can clearly see my spirit had darkened to the*
> *point where the flesh had taken control. I was*
> *descending into a void; Fast approaching a darkness*
> *I'd never before known; Teetering at the edge*
> *of an abyss; The very gates of a living hell...*

THE INSTITUTE
CARIMUM, TROMBETAS RIVER
April 18-28, 2005

Monday, April 18, 2005

I have great expectation going in to the days ahead. I certainly need some good company.

I've spent the last 11 days on my own. Can't remember a single second that I wasn't trying to drink myself to death. I've avoided the phone and refused meetings with people I should have met with. I feel totally defeated.

I came early to take care of some of the details around the Summer season. All I've done is drink myself silly. Zeek has picked up the slack as best he could. Bless him. S coming aboard didn't help Zeek and me at all. She's been on the boat almost since I arrived. Just wanted to see her. Needed to have some intimacy. She's always good for that. But Zeek thinks I should keep women away from the boat altogether. Thinks it's dangerous for people to see me like I am. It was a relief to see her go last night.

I'm feeling ok physically. But the weight of my actions this past week have trashed my soul. At the moment, it wouldn't matter if I lived or died. I think I'd much rather die. Don't know how to fix any of this. Can't imagine facing Vic again when I go home. The secrets from here are far too many and damaging. Just have to keep my mouth shut. She knows anyway. You know what though? *She* left *me*. Screw her...

After a night of airport runs to pick-up Jacobi (another brother-in-law) and Dad, we all ended up just sitting around waiting on Zeek to get the *Laura* ready. Frustrating time indeed.

Finally got all the food items, water, etc., onboard at about 5 this afternoon. Then, the main A/C in our cabin simply died.... The repairman couldn't make it out to check on it until 6:30. When he finally did show up, the news didn't come as a shock at all – the compressor had burned up. So, I sent him over to the *Belatis* and had him pull one of ours off the roof and install it over here.

Had a scare with Dad this afternoon. As he was arriving on the *Laura*, he stepped off the *WilPhilMatt* and fell flat on his face. His nose is a mess – red and swollen. My main concern is his thin blood due to the coumadin he takes. I watched him pretty closely for the rest of the afternoon. No sign of internal bleeding – Thank God.

Well, under a terrific rain and wind storm, we were fueled and underway by 8:30 PM. No sooner had we rounded the bend at the Tropical Hotel, the winds and waves got dangerously hostile. We had slowed to an idle and the *Laura* was rocking and rolling. I finally went to dad and suggested we find a safe harbor and call it a night. No sense in getting nowhere at all, in the middle of the night, while getting beaten by the winds.

My Dad, Me and My Brother

Tuesday, April 19, 2005

Underway at 3 AM. I didn't get up until 4. But, my brother is like clockwork. The pain he feels in his feet and ankles wakes him nightly. I wish there were something that could be done. All the meds that he has been taking (Vioxx, Celebrex, etc.) have been pulled off the market. We just don't know what to do. I just pray God will heal him – medicine has simply quit working. I've given him all the morphine I had in my bags. Surely it will help.

You know, yesterday I wrote a couple of page discourse on my reasons and challenges for being on this trip. I went in to a great deal of detail about the searching that I am involved in to seek out God's will for my life. I'll not attach that piece of "literature" to this log but will venture to plug in bits and pieces where they fit.

I guess for now, all I need to say is that God has convicted me that He wants something more from me in this life. He has been very clear with me that He has been trying to get my attention and get me to listen to Him for many, many years – I have just been "moving too fast" to take the time to listen. It is obvious that the difficulties that I have had in my life have been largely due to my own actions – *not* the attacks of Evil. I think blaming Satan for everything is pretty much weak, bullshit. We tend to charge "Satan", family members and circumstances with just about everything wrong that happens to us and the happiness that eludes us. Well, Evil is truly here and waiting to assist us in remaining miserable. However, it is *not him* or *family* or *other circumstances* that keep me, personally, in disarray. The main culprit in my life's story has been my own blindness. I still can't see what I should be seeing. Well, I am now 45 years old. My life is filled with responsibilities and seemingly has direction. But now, God is saying to me that I have missed the mark somewhere. I was talking and on the run when I should have been sitting quietly while He spoke to me. Right now, I'm uncomfortable, to say the very least. If He is going to say something to me, it needs to be soon. I'm fading fast.

I am using this Institute to have time with Dad, my brother and Jacobi. I know that God will bless me in my sincerity. I just want to have the peace of knowing that I am not only doing "good works" in His Name but that I also am doing it because it is what He has called me to do with my life. I have focused on the "good work" to cover all the shit inside me. I feel like a farce.

It is 5:40 and just my brother and I are awake. Daybreak is about here – the start of a new day. This is the first morning, in a *long time*, I haven't had a beer by now… Lord, give me patience and an open heart for today's cruising and visiting. It is going to be a long one… ETA for Oriximina is set for 10 tomorrow morning.

It is 7:15 and I'm just gazing out the window of the *Laura*, watching the riverbank go by and thinking of how things might have been if I had been closer to home over the years. Would my boys have turned out as good as they have? Would my Vic have been different in the way she views life? Would I be different in the way

I view life? Would I, at 45, be *seeking* at a time when most folks are content with their individual ruts? I really don't know – but today is going to be a good day. I look forward to it.

The *Laura* has just gone through a *total* remodeling job. It has been raining non-stop since we started our trip last night. Now we are seeing the leaks, etc., that were overlooked. When my Dad and brother return to Manaus, she will go back to the drawing board. Oh well, it always takes a "maiden voyage" to get everything working right.

It's 8:40 AM. We are in the midst of another big, bad storm. We finally made it in to the Parana da Eva. We are floating off-shore from Wellington's house right now. Just talked to him on the radio –all seems well with him and the family. Rains this time of year are a bit out of character. We are taking a beating for sure. Just wish we could have some smoother sailing.

Just got a call in to Vic on the Sat-Phone. All is well there. Tomorrow she goes in for some medical test. Before I left Minas couple of weeks ago, they found some abnormal cells on her cervix. Going to do a biopsy to see what is up. You know, it is quite reasonable to be anxious about these exams. I am concerned for her and the boys anytime there is illness. But, she has lashed out at me over this one. She's *immediately accused me* of bringing a *disease* back to her from my "adventures", as she describes these trips. I have *never* screwed a whore. I have *never* had a relationship with an unclean woman. Maybe she should just look at *her own* "adventures" for the source of whatever might be wrong with her, if anything is wrong at all. Man, just wait for the tests to come back...

Well, now all of us have had a shot on the phone with those back home. They're all well without us and *we* are still weathering the storms on the Mighty Amazon. This year, the river is predicted to rise to its 3rd highest level **ever** – an amazing 90 feet (normal is 45 – 60). Downtown Manaus is expected to flood for the most part.

I hope and pray that our trip destinations will suffer little from these ramifications. At least the volunteers won't have many hills to climb to get to location...

Dad just woke up. Good to see him. I sat everybody down after dinner last night and shared a bit of my anxiety with them. At the end, I let them know I would be having a few drinks here and there during this trip. I just don't feel "chipper" enough to fake it for this long. They responded with silence. I took that as an o.k....

It's noon and I just got up from the lunch table. Had some great fish (Dorado) and rice – couldn't ask for more. We are approaching Itacoatiara – already in sight. Half-hour away. This city has a lot of history with me. One of the meanest stretches of the Amazon River. Strong currents. I will pass by here a number of times this  summer with our groups, just as I've done for the last 20 years. It is the first "milestone" on our way to just about everywhere we go. Twenty years. How amazing. My secretary sent me some stats she'd complied a few months ago. I have taken 177 trips involving well over 3,000 volunteers into these waters since founding the Organization in 1986. My God. I know one day I'll look back and see a lot of beauty in it all. Right now, I just see what it's cost me deep inside. I've never been right in it. Don't really know why. A lot of inconsistency in what I have "preached" and what I've genuinely felt inside. It's got to change on a fundamental level for me to continue on...

I have been in rather deep thought this morning. I have been growing more and more anxious about what God may be going to do in my life over the next days and months. I feel a rather sick need to actually *know* what He is going to do. At the same time, I feel a strange peace about watching it all unfold. Odd spot I find myself in right now – Oh well….

Had a great visit with Dad and my brother this afternoon. It got a bit heated at times but was made up of things that needed to come out and be explained. Mine and my brother's drinking was pretty much at the head of things. My brother is more subtle with his shit. He "medicates" more than he drinks these days. Pisses me off that he's found a way to live without watching his breathe around people. But, the crap he's taking has never worked for me. To each, his own…. As a result, we are all hopeful of how God's Will will be unfolded to each of us over the next 10 days. 10 days to a *much*, needed miracle…

It is 6:10 PM and we are waiting on Serafin to get dinner put up for us. Gonna be steak and eggs. Sounds good and I am tire. It has been a *very* long day today. Much accomplished in my mind, heart and soul. I'm ready for it to end though…

Wednesday, April 20, 2005
Slept for an extremely long time last night. I lay down at 8:30 and just went pretty much straight through to 5:30 this morning – Evidently I needed it.

We past Parintins at 3 this morning which puts us on schedule for arrival in Oriximina at 10 AM. We are hoping that most of the 56 students of the Institute will already be there so that we might be able to cruise straight to Carimum and get settled into the environment there.

I have a seemingly serious meeting that must take place between me and the remainder of my affiliate's mission, board of directors. We have to get this Organization moved to Manaus; Membership altered; Hospital sold as well as the property in Obidos. Mainly, I just need for the Lord to take hold of the meeting so that we can get it all done with no personality problems.

I just read the book, in English, that Dad will be teaching at the Institute in Portuguese. It is called "The Nature of a God-Sent Revival", by Duncan Campbell. The book is nothing like I expected. It deals with the subject of revival as I have never seen it done before – I am no scholar but have heard much about spiritual revival. From what I gather from the simple reading of this publication, revival does not depend on the human factor, the amount of corporate prayer invested or the desire we have to see revival take place. We tend to confuse *Evangelism* with *Revival*. When we take the Gospel via evangelistic activities, we preach a *"come to Me and be happy"* message, rarely bringing about conviction, of any kind, to our lives. *Revival*, on the other hand, is an act *of and by God* that generates responses in mass, based on overwhelming conviction of wrong and the need of His saving grace. Shines a whole new light on our work in the Amazon and the way we maybe should be approaching our tasks.

Yes, we should be sharing the Gospel adamantly and fervently via all areas of the Organization's multi-ministry approach but, at the same time, be *dependent on God* to bring His conviction upon the masses. These are *two different ministries*. One for the body, which *we* are very good at, the other having to do only with *His* actions. Not necessarily one *leading* to the other. I'll have to listen hard these next few days to further understand or correct my views on this....

Just left Oriximina after a 5-hour halt in the trip to wait for some of the pastors to arrive – and arrive they did! We had lunch at Grace's restaurant. Jacobi and I found a "cyber" place to check our emails. I had nothing of great importance but was glad to be able to check anyhow. Liza is traveling so the meeting with my Brasilian BOD will have to take place next Wednesday at the end of the Institute. Just as well. Wasn't feeling up to it anyway...

Got to talk to William! I was trying to find Vic and *he* answered the phone. It is so good to hear the boys' voice when I am way out here. He is looking forward to the holiday. Today begins a "long" weekend.

Finally got to talk to Vic. She was very stressed. So, not much was discussed. The results from her medical tests will be ready on Friday. I know she won't be in a good mood until we know something concrete. The boys leave for a weekend church camp tomorrow. Maybe some peace and quiet will calm her a bit. I truly hope so. It is 6 PM and we are entering a storm as we travel. Looks very nasty and we have 22 of our pastors onboard. Hopefully, things will calm down quickly. Three storms in 2 days – I believe I've had enough... Not far behind us is the *Elvie* vessel. She, too, is carrying 22 pastors. Lord, please keep watch over them as I know You will. The *Elvie* is such a tiny boat...

The Good Lord willing, we will be in Carimum in another hour and a half. Then we will get the pastors settled on land and have our home "vessel" back to normal. I've just spend the last hour avoiding everybody as best I could. Been sitting in the hold, sipping a drink. Too hot down here to enjoy...

Thursday, April 21, 2005
Arrived in Carimum last night at about 7:30. The other pastors were 2 hours behind us. All were safe in harbor and a good meal in our bellies by 9 PM. I called it a night about then.

It was great to see all these pastors from the field. Many, I have not seen in several years. Others, I had never met. Good to see them all though.

Woke up at 4:00 this morning. I guess I'd had enough sleep. I took a couple of alprazolam's washed down with a single, tall drink last night. Seemed to work ok. Got up half hour ago and made some coffee. My brother just rolled out of bed too. Bless his heart, he doesn't look good. The pain he feels in his body has aged him considerably over the last months. His face is lined and his teeth seem to continually grind. Wish there was something I could do. I picked up some more morphine in Oriximina. Will dole it out to him as he needs. He's sitting out in the kitchen of the *Laura* doing some writing as I sit here in the cabin writing in the dark. I love the *Laura*. Her new design is comfortable. However, at 4 in the morning, with six people onboard, it is indeed hard to find a spot to sit, think and write without waking *somebody* up. It will be daybreak in an hour or so though. Gonna be an interesting week.

You know, I really don't want to sit here in the dark and write anymore. So, I think I'll pray awhile until the sun comes up... There will be more time for writing later this morning. The boat will be empty. I'll have some privacy.

Well, I laid back down again, instead. My mind wouldn't let me sleep. I don't know why this happens at times. It seems that my mind reels with memories, thoughts and, sometimes, bizarre anxieties. It's still just 5:30 but the thought of any further rest is discarded. Within a couple of hours, breakfast will have been served and the Institute will be in full swing. Lord, prepare me to receive from You – it is truly what I need today.

Went onshore for breakfast at 7. Everybody on land seemed to have gotten a good nights' rest. I feel badly about eating from a different menu than the rest of the crew though. Grace simply insists that Dad, my brother, Jacobi and I eat, separately and more abundantly. I am uncomfortable with this...

The study was great. This morning was just an introduction to both materials that will be taught. I look forward to it though. I have 26 pages to read in the next 4 hours, but I look forward to what it will yield. The pastors seem excited about the subject matter as well. There is something about the notion of a "personal, spiritual housecleaning" that is appealing and desired by most any honest, seeking person. They are as excited as I am.

We are out at anchor right now – will head back in at two for a little more study with Dad on "Revival".

The afternoon ended up with a good meeting about the second coming of Christ. We have 49 pastors here and, therefore, about 40 different opinions on how this event will take place. Very entertaining...

After the meeting, one of the men was taking a shower. For some reason, he was standing on the toilet (some folks are just too short to reach the shower knobs I guess). Anyway, the porcelain toilet burst into a dozen pieces and in the process cut the man's heel pretty badly. Didn't have to stitch. But in the process of seeing what materials I have to work with, I found that I have no gauze. In the morning I will send for some bare essentials because, obviously, shit *does* happen.... I have everything I need to pull teeth but that's just about it.

Great service this evening. I left a bit early – just couldn't stay awake through two sermons on the same subject. It is 9 PM and I can barely keep my eyes open – so, I just won't try anymore...

Friday, April 22, 2005
Interesting night last night. I was awakened with a jolt at 10:30 with a knock on the cabin door. One of the pastors from the institute was sitting in the doorway of the *Laura*, with about a 4-inch gash in his forearm. This guy was bleeding all over the place! Guess what, he was taking a shower after church, slipped, fell and cut himself on the same broken toilet seat the young man had busted earlier today!

To reduce a 30-minute ordeal down to a few words, I put 7 stitches in him and sent him home. I think we need to examine "showering" procedures at our next group meeting – get this new, *flesh slashing* tradition, under control. I hate to wake up like that. It's dark and quiet. My mind starts up again and I need to settle it. Went through a half bottle of scotch before finally passing out again. At this rate, I'll need to re-supply before long. Don't want to do that...

The studies went well this morning. I believe that the conviction of the Holy Spirit is beginning to descend upon some of us. We dealt a lot with "personal" cleansing – confessing our deepest darkest sins to God, as a first step toward being usable in His work. The confessing of my sins to God is not the main problem – I feel I have most always done this. The problem abides is the fear associated with the changes that must come about as a result of this confessing. These changes affect every imaginable aspect of our lives – be it family, ministry, friendships finances, etc.

I realize that I am being redundant to myself here. It is just such a *genuine* fear in my heart. My prayer, from now until God answers, is going to be that God remove these fears and give me peace with whatever changes will *necessarily* come to my little world. *Surely*, He will honor this request...

Just came onboard after lunch. I have had a number of requests for "medical and dental" assistance. I really want to help. However, in my helping, I and those I help will possibly miss part of what we are really here for. I believe that maybe I should just handle the emergencies as they come up. I don't feel comfortable with setting up "shop". Lord, just lead me and I will follow.

On a personal note, everybody here seems to be able to just lie down and take a nap in the afternoons. Here I sit writing to myself. I wish I could just lie down and sleep for a couple of hours – take a break from the world, so to speak. Just not in my metabolism, I guess. I have to medicate to relax and sleep. I envy these guys with nothing substantial on their minds...

Getting ready for to go to dinner. Looked at my "cut victims" a little while ago, after the afternoon study session. Both looked great. The one with the stitches looked extremely well – thank God...

Grace just got back from Oriximina with a new toilet bowl and some gauze for me. She also brought me two bottles of gin I'd left at her house a while back. Don't remember doing that at all. Glad I did though. It was wrapped in a towel, mixed in with some supplies. Don't believe she knows it was in there. If she did, I don't believe she would have brought it. She has taken care of me during many a stupor over the years. She says she's prayed for me a great deal. I've told her I've quit. Bless her heart. Anyway, we will put some *definite rules* in place about the use of the new toilet! As for the gauze, I guess it's a sign I need to pull some teeth at *some* point during the Institute...

The services were again good this evening. The two that preached were my kind of guys – one preached for 15 minutes and the other one ran out of steam in just 5. It was the first time for each behind the pulpit. Bless their hearts; I know how tough it was on them.

I lingered behind and visited after the service with several of the pastors. I really enjoyed the fellowship. They have so many hopes, dreams and plans. It was humbling to listen to them as they talked to me about it all. I miss those days, if I ever truly had them. It's been a long, long time since I've felt hopeful about my world. Surely it's not the way it should be. I know there is a better way. Searching...

Saturday, April 23, 2005
Got to bed at 11 and didn't wake up until 6 this morning – very rested – no alcohol last night. Dad had a rough night with diarrhea and fever. Of course, he didn't wake anybody up to help him. He is going to stay in this morning until he feels strong. There is a "bug" going around in this area. Flu-like symptoms. 48-hour deal. Dad should be ok by tomorrow.

Jacobi will take the lead this morning and do the evaluations of the services last night, etc. Jacobi is really enjoying himself. Nobody knows who he is – he is free to teach and fellowship. Back home, he is the president of the Pastor's Council for the Brazilian Baptist Convention and several other "impressive" titles. Here in the boonies, he is just "Pastor Jacobi" – he likes it this way.

It was a blessed morning. I learned more truths from our studies. It is going to take a good while to assimilate all that is taking place, but God is at least showing me clearly where I need to begin. This is all good. I am thankful for it. God is giving us all a great deal of spiritual food. I am digesting  it as eagerly and quickly as I can. What the other 49 pupils are doing is not my responsibility. I trust they are doing the same.

Dad did well this morning. He was rested and spoke with a strong voice. We are out here on the *Laura* now after the lunch hour. He doesn't have to go back till 2 PM. Rest is really all he needs. His symptoms tell me he has a little fatigue going on. Rest will do the trick. Started him on Cipro for his stomach. More for my benefit than his...

This afternoon's session was quite an experience. Dad decided to stay in and let a couple of the "senior" pastors do the teaching. Well, these senior pastors don't see eye-to-eye on practically *anything* other than the gospel message. So, what was to be a 15-minute outline study on the Second Coming of Christ turned in to a 2 ½ hour debate! Very comical for the most part. These guys were literally arguing over punctuation in the verses!! Oh well. Tomorrow Dad will fix things up. The "rookie" students are now thoroughly confused about the 2nd Coming and, quite honestly, so am I! Even wondering if He came the first time! Hahaha!

Its 6:50 PM and we're under a heavy rain storm. Tonight's service will be led by students with a bit more experience than those last night. We may be in for a marathon on the 2nd Coming of Christ – Oh, goody...

Well, it's 10 PM. The day is over. The service was beautiful. The preaching was a bit lacking (the two that preached tonight were trying to be "showmen") but there were several moving testimonies and special music that were uplifting. A very sweet spirited woman got up and gave one of the most beautiful testimonies I have ever heard in my life – nothing but thanksgiving; not a single requests of Him. After the service, I was taken to her to hear about her son. He was in an accident several days ago. The chainsaw he was working with "kicked back" and cut into his skull and nose. I will go to him tomorrow and see what I can. Reflecting on her spirit tonight, I considered myself and how I might react in her situation – I fell *way* short of the example she gave...

Sunday, April 24, 2005

Slept hard. Was up at 6 AM, not quite ready for the fresh day. Drank a half-bottle before finally passing out last night. Didn't really need any alprazolam but took a few anyhow.

At the study this morning, our theme was on telling the truth, *always* and being of encouragement to our fellows. The entire group, particularly me, came under tremendous conviction to ask for forgiveness to those that we have offended. It was like a huge weight lifted from my shoulders – I thank God for the opportunity to ask for forgiveness. For my arrogance and lack of humility in the past...

Left right after lunch with Gilberto and Jacobi to see a construction project over in Samauma Lake. Along the way, we visited Gilberto's house and the hut of the boy that had the chainsaw accident. God is truly good. The boy should be dead! Seems that he will recover completely though. I assured him that God must has something *very* special in store for his life and that he should be attentive to God's voice. It sure would have saved me some time if I had done so myself...

I dressed his wounds just as a storm rolled in. We all ran to another little hut nearby, to sit it. The lady of the house was a blessing to me. She served coffee and we gave the cookies that we had brought with us to the 15 kids that were in the room. We just sat around and visited for an hour or so while the rains came down – great time indeed.

Tremendous crowd at the service this evening. It is, after all, Sunday. Lots of visitors. The boy with the wound and the little girl with the facial sores, both came. It was good to see them and give them their meds.

Right now, for some reason, I just need to sit here and drink a little in the dark. It's been a good day. I've recognized some things in myself that made me uncomfortable, though. And it all seems insurmountable, somehow. How can a lot of people see things in themselves and just "change"? Who's really the simple-minded, fickle one here? Me or the rest of the world?

Monday, April 25, 2005

Slept a full 8 hours last night. Yesterday, on the way back from Samauma, we stopped at the home of a man that was in distress over a "wayward son" that is living in Belem. He shared with me that he was going to sell all he had to go and try to "retrieve" his son. I, uncomfortably under the circumstances, offered to purchase his boats. I can always use an extra

This morning, I took Dad over to see the boat. Like I said, I felt uneasy about even offering to buy the thing because of the *"why"* of the sale. Dad and I spoke with him for a good long time. In the end, he decided to call off all sales of his properties, go to Belem, try to bring his son back, then, leave it in God's hands. Thank you Lord for the wisdom and the experience. This has brought closer to home two truths that I already knew, but needed reminding of: **First**, never take advantage of a man's misfortune, or situations in the lives of others that may be helping them to make wrong decisions. **Secondly**, try to see a person's situation *prior* to negotiating – if what he needs is counseling or spiritual help, give that to him first. Then move forward *or* back out of negotiations.

This morning's study was on Sins in Relationships. Very moving and thought provoking. I have a lot to take home indeed – Lots to work on. My goodness, I've had more affairs in my lifetime than these guys would ever believe. The only "un-sinful" relationship I can ever remember having is probably with Vic. I'm a screw-up in the area of women. I just like them, a lot. Really though, I've just used them. Don't really know how much "like" was involved, if any. That's a whole another part of the picture I hope becomes clearer over the next couple of days. My, my, my...

Today is our day of fasting and prayer for Revival amongst us. I am unaccustomed to this type of activity but am willing to do it. I know that it is both Biblical *and* spiritually healthy, too fast. I trust God will move in my heart, in whatever ways He sees fit.

The afternoon's events went well. Dad's teaching on Revival was thought-provoking and induced a good deal of commentary regarding how the message of God's Judgment should be proclaimed.

The overall consensus ended up being that we should always preach judgment along with salvation. However, this should only be done if the preacher is under conviction that his heart is broken for the sinner that will face an eternity in hell should he not accept Christ's Gospel. It was very encouraging and refreshing to see the "fire and brimstone" preachers change their attitudes in how they view the lost world.

I have issues with the "fear tactics" used by most of these guys. I find it unnecessary and counter-productive, in most *all* situations...

I broke down and pulled some teeth late this afternoon. At least a dozen of the men at the Institute have asked me to take care of their teeth – I've been putting them off. Don't wasn't to get into it. Too shaky most of the time anyway...

Well, the day without food didn't seem to hurt anybody. I'm feeling tired earlier tonight than normal. I guess that's a good thing though.

Tuesday, April 27, 2005
Up at 6 this morning. Thought I would be starving to death. I was actually not hungry at all. The studies went well, as usual. It was also good to be able to sit down and have some lunch at noon. I didn't drink last night. Didn't seem appropriate with the "fast" going on. Had a tall one this morning though. Just had to...

Jacobi's study dealt with the Sins of Omission and Commission. Mind you, Jacobi teaches for a 3-hour period each morning, with only *one* 5-minute break in the middle – no one seems to notice the time go by – the material is amazing, gripping.

One of the things that really stood out to me was the fact that there are so many things in our lives that we literally have to "convince" ourselves that they are right things or *wrong* things to do. We do this every day. This is ludicrous! If we question something *at all*, it is either *wrong* or it is *right*. There is no need to ponder the situation. I don't need to question whether I should have had that drink this morning. I know it was wrong. However, I don't need to question why I took the drink, either. I took the drink because I needed the drink, thus making it right. See? I can twist words up as well. The "pope" isn't the *only* one that can play this game...

After lunch, Jacobi, Gilberto and I took off on another little trip to visit Batata to check things out for the Kentucky group. Great trip. I got a little sunburned but enjoyed every minute of it. A beautiful people there in Vila Batata. I had all but forgotten their faces, but as I visited, the memories came back – many memories.

The Laura

Took a bunch of pictures to send to Dwain B. This is going to be a great trip for Kentucky and the 8 communities we will work with.

On the way back, we took a little detour to see how the "chainsaw kid" was doing. He had already gone home with his mother. They live about an hour further up the creek than we went on Monday – not enough water for our johnboat to make it up that far. Maybe he will be at the church tonight.

Lots of folks came to church tonight. Unfortunately, most that came, came to see me – they or their children are sick. I didn't bring a bunch of meds on this trip. I only have personal stuff. I did what I could.

A disturbing fact was brought to my attention this evening. Of course, I am not a doctor or a dentist. However, I feel a very strong conviction to help as many as come to me, within the limitations of my ability and knowledge. I was told by several this evening that Mark Y., a physician, never helped a soul while he was down here on several Institutes of the past. To me, this is an abomination and a sin against both God and Humanity. May God have mercy upon the souls of people like that... What ungrateful misers of God's Gifts!

You know? My personal life is a mess right now. I don't feel very well, inside or out, most of the time. But, I would *never* refuse to help somebody within my capabilities. Never... Mark, you are a true S.O.B. Screw you, man...

Wednesday, April 27, 2005
Staid up fuming till the gin took effect. Should have stopped then, but I didn't. Drank an entire bottle of the gin Grace brought. By the time I passed out there was nothing more to think about. I needed that. Too much on my mind these days.

I awoke this morning with a strange sensation about me. I can't quite put my finger on it. I feel uncomfortable. Maybe it is the fact that this is the last day of the Institute. Maybe it is that I have a couple of surgical procedures to perform. Maybe it is the fact that I was unable to reach Vic yesterday to hear what her test results are. Maybe this, maybe that... I just don't know yet. Have to see how the day plays out.

The morning session was good. It dealt with "corporate sin" and "financial irresponsibility's" and the sins associated with it. Very relevant and soul searching. It dealt with tithing and accountability – I deal *much* in the area of accountability. The lesson today taught me to respect and welcome such accountability instead of rebel or belittle it. Very strong and good reminders to me about the whole issue – good material, indeed.

It is 10 AM. We've just finished with Jacobi's teachings. I tried to call Vic – she was sleeping. I trust she is just resting and relaxing after hearing that she is going to be well.

I believe the nature of my discomfort right now is that maybe, after all that has transpired in my spiritual life over these past days, I find myself in the position that I must go home and *act* on what God has shown me. This is not in any way negative – on the contrary, it is positive. It is, however, the source of a certain amount of heightened anxiety with which I feel uncomfortable.

Like I told myself earlier, I just need to see how this day plays out. Lord, give me peace as I complete the work I have committed to do today. There are bullets to be removed from the body of one guy and a delicate dental situation to resolve as well. Give us wisdom, grace and steadiness of eye and touch, dear Lord. You know better than any and all that my ability lays in Your capacitating, not our talent…

Finally got hold of Vic. Still no news.

The afternoon was taxing for me. Was shaking so much from last night. Had to have a couple of drinks to smooth things out a bit before leaving the boat. Really sucked to have to do that.

As the afternoon progressed so did the special requests for housecalls, etc. I snuck a huge glass-full and went ahead and did it all, until it was too dark to see. Thanks for the extra "cup" of grace, Lord.

Jacobi preached this evening. Good service and message. There was a young man there (46) that suffered a stroke a year-and-a-half ago, leaving the left side of his body pretty much dysfunctional. He had lost all self-esteem and self-worth. I treated him a couple of days ago and tried to encourage him. I gave him a Bible and a pair of my glasses. I found an extra pair in my dental stuff. He hadn't been able to read anything since his stroke, due to compromised, eyesight. His face beamed when he put on the glasses and began to read. Just one of those special moments that I will not forget for as long as I live.

Also, at the service, was the boy with the chainsaw wound. I could hardly believe it. The wound on his scull has completely closed! I took a picture of him just to prove it to myself. When I changed his bandage the other day, I must confess I was concerned for his life. Tonight, his wound just looked like a scratch on his forehead – unreal...

I'm tired tonight. The Institute is over for this session. I feel saddened by the fact. I have felt somewhat "safe" while here with all these good men. I have felt secure with Dad around as well. I know it's all about to end and I will be left to myself. Not looking forward to it at all...

Thursday, April 28, 2005
We are now headed for Oriximina. Departed from Carimum at about 5:30 this morning. I got up at 4:30, well rested. We are on our way home. I desperately tried to avoid drinking when I woke up. Was just feeling too shaky to face the day. What else is new. Just had a few fingers, though. Will try to manage the rest of the day just a "finger" at a time.

Arrived in Oriximina at 8:30. Went straight to the docks and bought our tickets to Santarem for tonight. The boat leaves at 9 PM. This should be a good experience for Jacobi. For those who have never ridden the line boats of the Amazon Valley, it is somewhat of a thrill. To me, it is simply the *only* way to get me to the airport to catch my plane home. Home... Other than the boys being there, not much to return to this time.

I've had time to think about home. The only time I see the boys is when I get them up for school. Usually, I've already had a couple of beers by the time I wake them up. Vic sleeps in and leaves right after she wakes up. By then, I've already had enough to drink and have laid down again. I get up, go out to the cabana and drink until the boys get home. The driver usually takes them straight away to the Club, for the rest of the day. I take a nap, get up and drink out by the pool again until I fall asleep at night. Don't even see Vic and the boys when they get in. It's a shame. Confusing. When I'm here, I do the same thing. Is there nothing else, God? Is this it? Why can I not see another way? Can't see another way. Please heal me. Please. I want to live...

Went up to the "cyber-café" in town and got online. To my relief, Vic was online too. I got her to open all my emails and send them through MSN. I was unable to open my mail from here. Lots of info – I'll get to responding all of it Sunday or Monday from home.

Vic got her results back from the doctor. Wednesday, she will have surgery to remove her cervix. I am glad we finally know the results and what needs to be done. I will be there to take care of her. Lord, use this as a *positive* thing in our lives. I am anxious and scared but know that the surgery is simple and, most of all, You are going to be right there with us, every minute.

Well, I guess I'll end all this right about here. Much more could be said of these days here on the Trombetas. But, no more needs to be said. Now, what I have learned must be lived out in my daily life, over time. I certainly need to abstain while at home this time. Really, really need to or theirs no deal. I'll have to leave the house. And, I *want* to stay at the house this time...

> *My Brother, whom I've mentioned throughout my Diaries, was in rapidly, declining health during these days. We would never again travel together. Within five months, he is dead, leaving five children and four ex-wives in his wake. Just a few more innocent victims, added to the millions that came before them. Victims of this relentless, unforgiving disease...*

I finally made amends to my brother at his gravesite in the Amazon Rainforest, in 2010. That experienced felt like far too little, too late. If only we could have found, together, the peace I would eventually find. We just didn't know it existed...

My Brother & Me...

CHAPTER TWELVE

*"We admitted we were powerless over alcohol,
that our lives had become unmanageable..."
Completely overwhelmed, I finally surrender to the
fact I can live no more in the way I was living. I had
no more 'ideas'; no more 'lifelines' to grab hold of; no
more 'excuses' for the human being I'd become. Only
a Power Greater than myself could restore me to
sanity. Only God could do the work needed for me to
survive. He would do so if I would but surrender...*

This was it. After all the 'bottoms' I had
experienced in the past, this was the final one.
I have just come out of a week-long, alcoholic 'black-out'. I can't recall any of the comfort I used to feel in the
company of alcohol and the women I was drawn to for
solace. Neither seemed to be working for me anymore.
In this final episode, I somehow know my stint in
hell will end. It has to. I can live no more as I had
lived. Something new will have to emerge from out
of the darkness or my life will simply slip away.
I know God put Mike in my life a couple of years
prior. Today, I see him as an 'angle' God sent to show

the Path. Mike, of course, would probably prefer to be referred to as my first 'Sponsor', instead...

RIVER NHAMUNDA/ALABAMA TEAM
July 27-August 04, 2006

Friday, July 28, 2006
Yesterday was a long, long day. The group arrived pretty much on time, but without a single suitcase or action packer. So, we waited all day. I didn't get a wink of sleep. My mind was reeling a bit about home, the trip, family, etc. I just stayed up until it was time to go and see if the bags came in at 1:30 this morning – they did indeed arrive. We sat around for several hours at the airport waiting for Customs to clear everybody, then we went in and got our 41 pieces.

Before we went to the airport, Mike and I sat and talked for a couple of hours about this and that. We finally got around to my drinking. He just grinned and said he'd been waiting for this day for a long time. Come to find out, he hasn't had a drink in 21 years. Impossible... He suggested I go to a place in Birmingham to detox from the sedatives in my system. I didn't argue. Don't have the strength or desire to argue anymore.

These last 12 days have been hell for me. I started drinking the minute the last team left the boat. I knew I wouldn't want my boys around to see any of the fall out, so they didn't arrive from the USA until Wednesday to join me on this trip. I now feel horrible about that. I really wanted them by my side. I guess I wanted to drink more. Freakin pathetic. I can't do this anymore. I am dead inside. I weighed myself at the airport when I dropped the last group off. I'm down to 137 pounds. What a cluster-bomb of days that must have followed...

I'm trying to remember everything, but for the life of me, I can't. I know that both V and A met me at the hotel when I arrived from the airport. These women have been pretty steady company to me all year. But, *never* both at the same time. Don't really know how it came about that they were *both* with me. Just remember them leaving last Tuesday night – 7 days later. I know Zeek must have stopped by to drop off beer and whatever the ladies needed. I only know *this* because I guess we never ran out of anything. Other than that, and a nurse at the hotel kindly plugging me up to an IV on Tuesday before I returned to the boat, everything is a blank. It feels like I went to sleep the first night and didn't wake up until a week later. Damnnnn...

I called Dad at 4:15 this morning to let him know the bags had arrived. He had been praying hard – *his* prayers, at least, go high...

It is 8:15 AM and most of the *Belatis* is asleep. I just talked with Vic – She sounded good. I hope she has a good "1st day of being 40 years old". Happy Birthday, honey. Since we've been separated this time, we have spoken very little. I don't blame her in any way. She should have left me the day she met me 18 years ago. With the exception of the boys, *no* woman deserves what I have given her. Bless her heart...

The sun is hot this morning, but there's a cool breeze to compensate. It seems like it will be a good day for cruising. Phillip got the *Phillip* out of the shop yesterday, late. The throttle control had broken so he decided to just put in the best one available (a Morse Control). He's excited about using it, I'm sure. There will plenty of opportunity this trip. I really want the boys to have a great time on this last trip of the year. As for me, I'm done in more ways than one. After this trip, I can head on home for a bit before going to Houston, Minnesota, Kentucky and, ultimately, Birmingham now that I've spoken with Mike.

It is 3:50 PM and we are approaching Itacoatiara. Just got a call from Edno in Urucurituba. There is a man there that some eye surgery was done on that's ulcerated. We are going to re-do the surgeries on both eyes. I just hope he travels with us so that we don't lose time. Whatever the situation, it will have to be done... I know exactly what happened though. He went back to work and lifted some kind of heavy weight in the process. I just wish these people would obey the post-op orders the doctor's give them. Now, we have to re-work somebody else's work. We don't like to do this kind of thing.

In the meantime, Matthew and several of the crew went in to Itacoatiara aboard the tender, T&T to pick up some things for the kitchen. Matthew was wanting to look for some DVD's to watch on these long hauls to and from destinations. Bless his heart; he gets so bored when he has to cruise for 2 days to get to work! He's just like me...

A huge storm just brewed. After a pretty good struggle against the wind and rain, we made it to shore and tied off. I was lying down at the time it all started. When I got up, I realized that my "wonderful" crew simply waited too long to seek safe-harbor. I have instructed them that the *first sign* of a wind building, they are to dock immediately. They will learn soon that I mean what I say.

It is 6:34 PM and we just got underway after **another** storm brewed. This time the crew pulled over at the very sight of the oncoming situation. That's the way I like it to be.

Underway Again...

I sent Nonato and Silvio out to look for some fish to buy. They found 2 Surubim that weighed right at 35 pounds apiece – going to be good eating for sure. Everyone has just had dinner. I want to hurry up and get to Urucurituba so we can do the surgery on this guy's eyes and get underway again. We are taking a very long time to get there. I would just love to get to the Nhamunda cut-off by sunrise. It would make me feel we have made up a little bit of time....

Saturday, July 29, 2006
5:24 AM and we just entered the 'pass' 30 minutes ago. The crew forgot to wake me up on time, but I made it on my own at 4:30. This is another "early riser" group. So, it is going to be important that my boys not forget to wake me.

I feel a little better than I did yesterday. The body seems to be trying to recover. But, my mind and soul are not doing well at all. I have no alcohol on the boat this time. I hope the sedatives do their magic until I can function again. At least function...

The water is much lower now than it was a few weeks ago. We have already run aground once but pulled ourselves off with no problem. I trust the levels will hold until we come out next week...

Our eye patient bailed on me last night. He re-scheduled for Maues if I come back through in mid-August. I hate that he did that, but I was very tired any way. Don't know we could have done an hour of micro-surgery anyway. I have a pretty constant tremor in my right hand right now. Just pay-backs I guess.

My boys are up with me right now. It may be a sign of how the future might look. Now I can finally share in how my own father must have felt through the years as my brother and I traveled with him through the lakes and rivers of this great Valley. Wow...

Picked up Edno, Abraao and his wife, Val, in Urucurituba. It was good seeing them. ETA is set for Nhamunda at 9 AM. I starting to look forward to the days ahead. Just hope my body and mind become more adaptive as the days unfold. Right now, I'm having difficulty feeling excited about anything at all.

Arrived in Nhamunda on schedule but went straight to Jurua to pick up Julio. He was not there... We waited out a storm, then took out toward Portuguese. I simply cannot understand a man like Julio. He *never* does what is asked of him. He always puts on a good show that breaks everybody's hearts – but, it is a smokescreen in my eyes. I have had enough...

I have been extremely anxious today. Alabama is the *only* group that I have any problems *at all* with the Itinerate Pastor on the field. They do not deserve this and neither do I. I've wanted to make changes on the Nhamunda River for two years – now, it must be done.

We arrived in Portuguese at 4 this afternoon. The adults and children were in true, beautiful form. They came down the hill with banners and signs, singing and cheering. These people are the best – I love them dearly.

As soon as the gangplank was halfway in place, I went down and found Julio in the crowd and we "took a walk". Same excuses as ever – we were late, he was concerned. So, he grabbed his family and came up here yesterday. I was very controlled (I know people were praying for me) but blunt and angry. I informed him that his boat and family would be taken back to Jurua and Edno and Abraao would take the boat from there, tomorrow. He, of course, said that would be fine. He would continue the trip with us on the *Belatis*.

On Shore...

This has all been very difficult for me these past days and weeks. I've been the "king of lies" and "smooth talk" for many years – I can spot one with no problem at all. Julio is pathological in this area. Lord, give me strength to stand firm with my decisions. It is better to have no one at all in this area than to have this man.

Got most everything up on location this afternoon. Visited with Mr. Luis and Socorro for a bit then, pulled out to anchor. I had a hard time with dinner. I ate but my stomach was in knots. Mike came and spoke with me a bit and helped with some advice about "honey" and "sweet things" I may be needing during this incredible hangover. He is such a fine man. I owe him in a big way. I just trust I can repay him someday.

Went back to shore at 7 PM for the church service. There were so many people that we had to move to an outdoor setting in the middle of town. It was a great evening. Many presentations by the children and adult groups. I was very much moved. A good ending to a very hard day.

Sunday, July 30, 2006

Nonato got me up at 4 AM with my coffee. Today will be a big day – the only day here in Portuguese. I slept well but am not rested.

Last night, when we all got back to the boat, Edno and Abraao came to me and were very emotional in a request for me *not* to take Julio's boat away from him. Julio definitely got to them – they fell right in to his emotional trap. I was very tired and it was quite late but, I gave them Julio's history and the *real* story of what was going on. They then agreed with me. Julio actually lied to them yesterday afternoon right after I had spoken to him. He told them he knew *nothing* about them taking the boat today – I had confirmed this with him just a couple of hours prior to that. Today is going to be a "day" for sure. I just need to get all of it done as quietly as possible. Everybody on the *Belatis* loves Julio (including me). But, he needs to be handled – *today*...

My coffee doesn't taste right and I don't feel chipper at all. I have to handle all of these situations ASAP in order to feel right. It is 5:15 and I can't wait to get on shore – I have to get all of this done and right or I can't be what I need and want to be to everyone that needs me today. I need to be free of this deal right away, for my own sake. I don't feel well as it is. This just adds insult to injury.

The *Belatis* is coming alive – it's 5:25. I'm not sure if I need to go on to shore at sunrise or wait till the *Belatis* goes in at 7:00. I'll just wait and see. I just got the boys up. I am going to miss them terribly when they leave. I need to keep that fact in my mind and heart.

Before the Belatis Wakes Up

As soon as we came ashore at 6:45, I took Julio on another walk to settle things. I took Abraao with me to make sure I had a witness to what took place. Well, I went straight to the point regarding our conversations of the night before, etc. Julio simply lied to me again, saying he must have misunderstood me. Abraao was flabbergasted – he couldn't believe what he was hearing! To make a *long* story *very* short, the boat will leave when I decide it will leave and that will probably be tomorrow from Sao Francisco…

Enough of this saga. Now, on with the day…

All teams were very busy. Construction had an insurmountable task to perform (as we well knew they would). They laid a very wide footer around the 3 principle sides of the church building. The rains had washed out and undermined the foundation. In doing this, the team actually completed the most critical part of the entire wall raising. All the locals will need do is come up with the walls on top of the footer. A fantastic day's work for our team!

Dental and medical were very steady, all day. Dental had a couple of challenges and medical performed a couple of emergency procedures. VBS did a GREAT job dealing with the huge number of children! Eye glasses were also given out by the dozens and dozens. We also did the "Lady's Ministry". I always love doing this! All the women get a kick out of me being the only man in the room and translating in the 1st person as if I were a woman also... We all have a great time with this each year. It is a vital ministry to these lovely women, and I am very pleased that Judy W. does it!

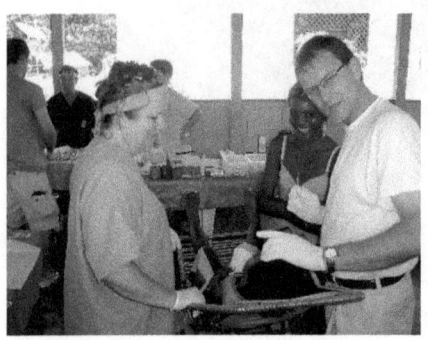

I am grateful to Doc Mark. We needed an extra interpreter in medical. He accepted Matthew! He was so patient and kind. I was proud of Matthew for stepping up to bat in such a dramatically different way for him. He fit the bill though. If Mark will allow, I will keep Matthew there the rest of the trip, if need be. It is a joy to see my boys developing in such fantastic ways. Few fathers that I know have such a privilege...

I tried to call Mom this morning. It was her 73rd Birthday yesterday and I had so much going on that I remembered it but, just didn't have time to call when I thought of it. I finally left a message on their answer machine – Dad must have taken her away for the day. Happy Birthday Mom!

By 5:00 PM, we had packed up and bagged out. The group and community gathered together out in front of the village to say our good-byes. It was a teary, touching experience. Socorro and a couple of other ladies gave gifts to the individual work teams and made some beautiful remarks. Everyone in the Amazon Valley knows that I love tucupi (manioc hot sauce). Well, I was given enough fantastic and fresh tucupi today (about 6 liters) that I won't need any more for the rest of the year! It was a good ending to our time here. I hope to come back again someday...

Underway for Sao Francisco at 5:45. ETA is set for 7:30 PM.

Monday, July 31, 2006

Up at 4 AM. Feeling very rough. I was craving a drink so badly. I was dizzy and could barely sit up in bed. Shaking like a leaf. I went ahead and to 2 mg of Alprazolam. Had to sit on the bed for half-an-hour before I felt stable enough to try getting up. Need to tell Mike about it. See what he thinks.

It's 7 o'clock now. We are anchored offshore of Sao Francisco. I'm feeling a little better and feel good about the day ahead. My body is still trembling inside. All groups ashore by 8 this morning. It was a rough morning – not what I had expected at all when the day started. There seemed to be strife everywhere. Julio's wife cursed me for taking their boat away from them. Evidently, Julio lies to her as well – I just told her she needed to work the reasons out with her husband – he has known them for a long time now... I can't help thinking of how Vic has had to live with me. I see similarities here. So sad...

The *Sandy* left port for Boa Vista do Ramos at about 2 this afternoon. It is somewhat of a relief. I just hate all of this stuff I have to do. I know it's part of my "job"; I will always hate it though...

Sao Francisco is a different kind of place. The people of this community are poor and somewhat lethargic. They, themselves, are a sweet people. The communities around them I have found to be evil, at best. I do not believe I have ever felt as oppressed in such a short period of time as I did today. I was badgered and lied to by practically everyone I came in contact with. They wanted "things" – anything we had. I was so angry and depressed by the end of the day, I wanted to scream but didn't have the strength to do so. I said some horrible things to a couple that I felt were trying to manipulate me. I feel horrible about it. Need to apologize to them…

Mike pulled me aside a couple times today and told me to let go and breathe. Don't know how he knew I was struggling. Guess he did, though. I've tried to hang around dental today just to be near him. This guy is special. Really special…

We had a short service at the end of the day. When it began, I confess I didn't want to be up front speaking to the people. I didn't feel good and was finding it hard to believe the stuff I was saying. know I *want* to believe there is hope in this life. I know it is there, somewhere. I just don't feel it myself right now and don't know how to achieve it.

We left Sao Francisco just before 6 PM. A small boat was dead in the water out by our anchor position. He had gotten tangled up in our anchor line and messed up his water intake and prop, as well as near severing our line. We toed the boat to its home (about an hour), fed the 12 that were onboard and got back on track for Aibi by 7:00. Lord, please end this day. I have had more than enough.

Tuesday, August 01, 2006
It is 3:15 AM. I can't sleep anymore. I was in bed by 8:30 last night. I have had enough rest I guess. I just wanted to get up and be alone for a while. I will try and call Vic and Dad this morning. I just need to hear some different voices…

Yesterday took a lot out of me – dealing with Julio, his wife, the people, etc. It is the kind of day when I question many things in my heart and mind. Mainly my mind. I try to turn things over to God, but I fail miserably. Well, today is another day. A day that I will determine to abide in the Lord and let him move through me.

I try so hard to show my boys how to be good leaders though my example. Days like yesterday, I simply chalk up to "bad" lesson days for them. guess it is important they learn that "bad days" do indeed come up. In reality though, I know in my heart I've shown them far more "bad" than "good". Don't feel like a father at all sometimes. Hope this can change someday.

On a funny note, from the beginning of the trip, there has been one of our team members that literally *everyone* has complained about. This person snores so badly that no one around her seems to get any sleep. So, we moved everybody around and put her up in my place and I stretched my hammock behind her. I slept all night. She *did* actually wake me up but not by her snoring – she woke me up to ask me if I was the one she heard coughing! Yup, that was me...

I pray this morning, Lord that You just keep me level headed. Remove the anger from yesterday and re-light a little joy along the way. I know this is something that I must ask for daily. Most days I just forget to start out that way. I know you are right here with me. I'm finding it hard to reach out and touch you. I feel ashamed to even try. I've screwed up badly with the life you gave me. I feel a long way from you...

Today will be a good day. I will not allow it to be any other way. With Your help and permission, Lord, surely we can make this day bright and alive.

It is 5:08 AM. The *Belatis* will begin to come alive any minute now. I guess it is time to shut down for now. Boyd, just be positive today – no matter what happens...

Aibi had a great reception for us as we came; children singing and holding up posters, etc. A very lightening thing for a heavy heart.

No sooner had we reached the shore and begun to see how our stations were set up, Julio asked if we could have coffee back at the boat – I was in agreement, of course. We spoke bluntly about his work and the direction it might take. He mentioned a new business venture involving a Jet Boat service between Terra Santa and various other large towns. I encouraged him vigorously. I further advised him that any other activity would mean becoming divorced from AMOR in every way but, would still help him by selling him the 85 hp Mercedes back at our dock – He understood. Now, we just wait for him to visit with his wife about it...

I called Vic this afternoon just to say hey and to find out about the Tropical Hotel reservations for this group. She has been working on the reservations and thinks all is well. The rest of the conversation was ridiculous. Seems she's found some of the writings, "confessions", I've made to myself on a laptop I left at home. I won't even go in to details because they are null and void anyhow. She is furious. What a nosy bitch. She's brought this on herself. How *dare* her look at my private stuff...

I called Mom and Dad just to see how they were making it. It was good to hear them. I need to get home to be with them for a bit. Feel I need to sit with Dad for a while. Would do me good.

Pulled offshore and anchored at 6 PM sharp. I'm not going to wait up for the snack. Just want to lie down. The day has been fruitful in many, many ways...

Wednesday, August 02, 2006

Nonato delivered my coffee to me at exactly 4 this morning. It was a cool night, but I managed to sleep quite well. No interruptions at all. I'm feeling stronger today. My mind is clearing. No thought of drinking. Not even wanting a sedative. We'll see how it goes...

Well, it is 5:05 and I am going to get Mike up for coffee. Start the day "breathing"...

I went ashore ahead of the team, at about 7:30 this morning. I met with the president of the community, the Catechist of the Catholic Church and about 10 other interested folks about what we're here to do. All seemed fine with them and they seemed delighted to have us. I looked around for the couple I met in Sao Francisco the other day and found that they did not live there. So, I hired a taildragger to go to where they live, find them and bring them to me. It is just *too* important that I see them...

The day went extremely well. The construction team literally built a house from the ground, up! By 5:15 PM, it was up and covered – unbelievable feat! VBS had a small group as did the Lady's ministry. The village is small... By day's end, everyone had been treated and ministered to. The couple I mentioned earlier finally arrived around noon. The tail of the tail-dragger that I hired to pick them up snapped its stem. So, I just gave him the one I had here onboard... turned out to be quite an expensive apology indeed. It just had to be done though.

The church service started right at 5:30. What a blessing it was! Bro. Terrance preached on the two gates again this evening. His voice is gone. I hope it is just superficial and not an indication of any kind of deeper throat problems.

When the invitation time came around, I just carried it along as the Spirit led – as always. Well, people began to respond to the Holy Spirit. They began to come forward. Then, the Catechist came forward and the president of the community stood and objected from where he was in the audience. He proclaimed that "...we are all Catholics here and we already know God." He wanted me to shut up right then and there. I walked closer to him and explained that these people were responding to the message Christ had died to spread. They were not committing to change "religions". Religion has nothing to do with what these people are responding to. He quieted down and people continued to come forward.

What an evening to remember. For the first time in all my years of sharing Christ, I think I finally understood the message myself, from my own mouth. Knowledge and ritual counts for *nothing* at all. There is a *relationship* to be establish. It is all about a relationship and nothing else. Wow...

Underway to Nhamunda to refuel and sleep for the night. Have no idea about an ETA and really don't care...

Thursday, August 03, 2006
Got up at 3:15 this morning. I feel light and rested.

Last night, I woke up as we were fueling the *Belatis* and buying a canoe for another tail-dragger we will probably end up giving away. I look forward to this last day on location. We will be in St. Maria – new territory for the second time this trip. I love it. We will arrive unannounced. I love that too...

It is 4:45 and I just woke up my captain to get us underway by 5:30 AM. Should be a nice 2 or 3-hour cruise...

You know, it is amazing how this trip has developed. We started out a day late and still got 5 full days on location with two brand new ones to boot.

We finally arrived on location at 10:30 this morning. After a brief lunch, we were all working by 11:30 – work till we're done.

Santa Maria is a unique community. It is large (about 60 families) and it became obvious to me, quickly, that it is a community mainly made up of prostitutes and the like. They make their living off of the folks that come to party on the weekends, etc. A very lively, yet depressed bunch of people.

As we went through the afternoon's activities, I could feel that God was going to act amidst the desperation all around me. I just felt a strange comfort in the fact that we were actually in the right place. I have never been here and neither had Julio and his bunch. No One at all has been here to share the gospel with these people, *ever*...

We finally started the closing service around 5:30 PM. When it was turned over to me near the end, I looked out over the crowd and could see little or no hope in the eyes of the people gazing back at me. So, I began to speak of my own battles with hopelessness and lack of guidance over the years – troubles and losses that have come my way. By the time I gave the invitation, the Holy Spirit had convicted 8 souls to reach out to Him. Anything I have been through and continue to go through that helps 8 souls come to know my Christ, is well worth it – one in exchange for eight? The math works...

After the services, it was time to make final arrangements with Julio. It was a time when, quite frankly, I had limited compassion.

However, I did more than I had originally planned to do. I gave him the Mercedes to start his business with and also agreed to pay him a month and a half's salary to get his children back in school. I know that I have made some people from our team pretty upset by letting him go. I'm sorry it had to happen right now, while they were all here – it just couldn't wait another day. All will be ok...

Friday, August 04, 2006
We got underway last night a little after 7 PM.

Just after midnight this morning, the *Belatis* ran aground. I woke up immediately and took the helm to free her. I have a good crew, but I have run aground more times than all of them, combined! So, I put the Jon boats in action in proper positions and we were free within about an hour. In the meantime, Loren was taken to sick-bay. She went down yesterday afternoon from overheating and hasn't been drinking hardly anything. Mark is going to give her until later this morning to start doing things right or he will hook her up to an IV for good measure. Fortunately, everyone else seems to be on the mend...

It is now 3:20 in the morning. After the "running aground deal", I was unable to go back to sleep. There should be time for a catnap later in the day if I need one... Right now, I thought I'd do some reflections on the trip and things in general.

I was able to visit a great deal with Mike before going to sleep last night. We spoke rather extensively about the task ahead; the various shoes that need to be filled all around for me to be able to step away for a while. We are going to call it a "sabbatical" so my BOD and teams won't be suspicious or concerned.

The primary decision we made was that I remain in the USA where an "anonymous fellowship" is readily available, in most any town, when I leave the detox center. He said the meetings they have will be essential for me and I should prioritize my days around the times they have them. He even says I might ought to stay away from the church for a while. That's kind of a relief. Don't much want to be around that environment. Strangely, I don't feel part of all that goes on there right now. Maybe never did. Mike says that's something that may come to me later. But, for now, I shouldn't be concerned with anything but these "meetings" and calling him every day.

This should all be good for my parents, too. Mom has gone into a deep depression after my brother died last year. She doesn't talk much anymore. Her memory seems to be fading, quickly. I've bought a house near them. It seems they will need me closer, more and more.

I don't have another trip down here until January of next year. It should give me time to follow as Mike leads in this new life he says is mine if I'm willing to put forth the effort. I am...

I still have several key business trips to make as soon as I hit home. I have meetings in Minnesota, Florida and Kentucky before heading to Birmingham. All of this within a month or two of my arrival. Plus, I need to formalize a new, extended Board of Directors for the Organization. My plate is pretty freaking full. Mike questioned whether I should do any of it before going to Birmingham. I think I convinced him that if I didn't make these trips *before* Birmingham, I would have little to return to *after* Birmingham.

I've decided to just give up. Mike says it is the first step to having any kind of life at all. I don't fully understand the concept but am fully willing to do so. I told him that I feel I've been living in a dark tunnel all my life, but I think I can see a tiny light at the end of it now. Somehow, I have no desire to drink at the moment. It feels rather strange, but I am grateful for it. He told me that the light I see, is "life" as it should be, and what we are about to do is try not to put it out. My, my. I want that more than anything in the world – always have. What a miracle that would be...

Mike says that I should approach my days in a different way. Experience them as if each one was the only one there was. Don't know exactly what he means by that, but he says that if I will follow his instructions for a while and not look any further into the future than "today", I will eventually know what he's talking about.

You know? I just want to be a "follower". I'm tired of leading people where I feel they need to go. I have failed miserably at it. Thank God it hasn't caused anymore tragedy other than, mainly, for me and my family. I feel horrible about my entire life. Mike says I *should* feel this way. Well, shit...

> During the course of this final entry, Mike was leading me to "Admit that I was powerless over alcohol, that my life had become unmanageable". This is but the 'first step' to be taken on the path to sobriety. It is also the only one that would need to be taken perfectly, without any reservations. The immediate road ahead will be difficult at best. But, from the final day of this trip forward, I will slowly begin to experience the " Sunlight of the Spirit" for the very first time in my life. A light never more to be snuffed out by alcohol, one-day-at-a-time... Through all the joy and heartache that is to come, I haven't found it necessary to take another drink. And for this, I am eternally grateful...

New Waters Await Us...

EPILOGUE

Alcoholism is a disease of the soul as well as the body. I am not an addict but will assume that most addictions function in much this same way.

As a disease, its all-encompassing nature makes it unique as to its needed treatment. Recovery from alcoholism depends on both spiritual and physical healing. However, emphasis must be placed on the spiritual in order to achieve sustainable remission.

With any given disfunction, the best to help with it are those whom have overcome it. Family, religion, psychiatry and psychology have proven to be lacking in this area. It's not their fault. When their efforts fail it is because of the alcoholics inability to be honest around his own dilemma. He or she is a master of manipulation, able to use these well-intentioned resources to 'buy some time'; put on a show of 'trying to get better'. In reality though, the alcoholic is just seeking sympathy and justification for continuing on.

The medical field is to be respected for what they are able to provide. By the time most alcoholics enter recovery, their bodies are in horrible shape. So much damage has been inflicted on tissues and organs that, without medical assistance, even death may be imminent. Many of us need professional help while detoxing. Those of us who have recovered, recognize the benefits of medicine in certain cases. However, we are quick to express caution over its continued use after the mind begins to clear. 'New addictions' must be avoided.

The treatment for alcoholism must be effective or the alcoholic will not recover or survive. Even though willingness on the part of the individual is imperative, the life-long treatment method must be strong and proven.

I became sober through the "worldly version" of 12-step programs. The 'original'; 'mother of them all'. The one established in 1935 by couple of drunks unable to achieve sobriety in any other way. The one gratefully housed in basement rooms of church annexes around the world today.

I, by no means, believe our fellowship has a monopoly on recovery from alcoholism. However, I've sponsored many who have failed in other well-intended, more 'sterile' environments. Maybe a quick story will express what I'm attempting to convey: **"While I was drinking myself to death between trips in 1993, there was a Catholic Church just across the street from the roach-infested room where I was staying. The bells started ring at 7 PM, announcing the Mass that was soon to begin. I prayed, in the midst of this stupor, that God would make me whole once again. So, I stumbled through the front door to a seat in the very back. It seemed dark and oppressive, but I was desperate and hopeful.**

"Soon, a young priest shuffled and tripped his way to the podium and began to speak. As he repeatedly bumped his mouth and head against the microphone, what proceeded from his mouth was summarily, unintelligible. Soon, a couple of 'alter-boys' came and mercifully led him away. I was distraught. God was simply not there. In my alcoholic mind, He had failed me once again...

"Thirteen years later, in my very first year of sobriety, I was seeking out meetings while between trips in that riverfront city. To

my surprise there was one that evening in the basement of that very church! How cool is that!? So I went.

"*Halfway through the meeting a man wearing a frock came in quietly, taking the seat next to mine. There was something familiar about him. As the meeting continued, I figured out who he was! At the break, I asked him if he was a priest in the church upstairs many years before. He answered, "Yes, and still am. However, the God I used to talk about up there I only came to truly know down here... I am sober today because of God's miraculous grace and provision though these rooms, not those upstairs".*

You see, In 1993 I had gone to the *right building* but used the *wrong door* seeking the help I needed...

When dealing with life-threatening illnesses, the proper diagnosis, treatment and environment must be applied. For the alcoholic, the diagnosis must be made by him or her themselves. The call for help must come from them. Once this 1st step is taken, treatment of the disease can commence. This treatment must be carried out with the help of those just like him in an environment of communality, unity and brotherhood. An environment with singleness of purpose and the resolve to live life differently and abundantly.

I speak in churches around the world regarding 'missions' and sharing Christ with a lost world. However, regarding alcoholics, I point them to the only path to Him that worked for me. Eventually, most who are fortunate enough to recover, find their way back to the church. But it's important to know that the church isn't the only place He may be found. As a matter of fact it is often the last place He will be sought by an alcoholic like me...

Church, if you want to help the alcoholic in your midst, consider providing a dark room in your basement for the 'worldly version" program of recovery. And don't worry, we won't smoke cigarettes in your bathrooms or be late with the rent. Our life depends on it...

TIMELINE

Chapter One
1999
Vic's ultimatum was clear: "If you are still drinking, don't come home..."

Chapter Two
1999
From 'building' to 'destroying' in just 12 days...

Chapter Three
2000
A 'double agent' joins our staff. Can't think of any better reason for having a drink...

Chapter Four
2000
"Is there something wrong in what we are doing or is it just the wrong in me that is disturbing? Both, it seems..."
I didn't understand it at the time, but I was beginning to question all human, dogmatic input to what Scripture actually said.

Chapter Five
2000
'If I really loved Vic and the boys, I'd simply not drink'. A more untrue statement has never been made. I simply didn't know how <u>not</u> drink...

Chapter Six
2001
"My wife leaves me because of my drinking. I drink some more and have an affair. Then I drink a lot more because my wife left me, and I had an affair."
No break in the clouds. Just another hurricane after every devastating storm...

Chapter Seven
2001
"Denominationalism is the culprit. I hate it and suspect God does too. Not even a drink makes me feel 'ok' about it all. But, I'll drink at it anyway..."
God is trying to guide me to simplicity. My mind and the Spirit within me are so clouded by alcohol and sedatives, I simply cannot see the Path to follow...

Chapter Eight
2002
"If this is what life is about, I'll need relief and escape from it, every day. No doubt about it..."
The 'haze' seems to be welcomed at this point. I have no desire or inclination to change.

Chapter Nine
2003
"Pray, work and drink. Then, drink while I pray and work. Next step: just drink – because. working and praying don't get the 'job' done..."

Chapter Ten
2004-2005
"How dark it is just before the dawn..."
A loneliness was descending upon me. One that only another alcoholic could recognize.

Chapter Eleven
2005
"I'll do it my way. It is the only way it will work, until it no longer does..."
We are at a Bible Institute. I no longer believe we should be 'preparing pastors' to engage in dogma. I am broken. There is no way out. I am all but through questioning my thoughts and actions. The end seems near, and I welcome it.

Chapter Twelve
2006
"We admitted we were powerless over alcohol, that our lives had become unmanageable..."
Completely overwhelmed, I finally surrender to the fact I can live no more in the way I was living. I had no more 'ideas'; no more 'lifelines' to grab hold of; no more 'excuses' for the human being I'd become. Only a Power Greater than myself could restore me to sanity. Only God could do the work needed for me to survive. He would do so if I would but surrender...

OTHER BOOKS BY THE AUTHOR

When the 'bottom' has finally come and recovery begins, new life, perceptions, adventures, and calamities, necessarily follow.

'Not drinking' is but the necessary beginning. Learning to live through Spiritual growth now takes precedence over all else.

This journey continues in **"The Diaries & Writings of an Alcoholic Missionary : *The Sunlight of the Spirit*"**. Look for it on Amazon & Kindle Books, soon.

"The Diaries & Writings of an Alcoholic Missionary: *The Kaapu Diaries"* will fascinate the reader with tales and stories of life deep in the Amazon Rainforest. True stories of a mission little has been said about due to its secretive nature. Don't miss it. The journey in sobriety continues soon, on Amazon & Kindle Books.

www.thealcoholicmissionary.com

ABOUT THE AUTHOR

The **"Diaries & Writings of an Alcoholic Missionary"** were, originally, never intended for publication. These are personal accounts of how Boyd Walker lived and experienced his life. The writings were for him alone. He suffered intense and relentless pain for more than 25 years due to his alcoholism. These diaries are a record of his attempt to live duplicitously between heaven and hell. They begin in active alcoholism and continue into sobriety. As of the date of this publication, by God's Grace, Boyd has been sober for 13 years.

Boyd is a Christian, concerned *only* with the Simple Truth of the Gospel Christ made possible and commanded each of us to share. He is conservative in his theology, however, is not aligned with any established religion and is non-denominational in the pursuit of fellowship with other Christians.

He still lives in South America, dividing his time between an isolated indigenous tribe, deep in the Amazon Rainforest, and at home with his wife in Southern Brazil. They spend as much time together as schedules permit.

They have no children together, but enjoy a total of four sons, a daughter and three grandchildren between them.

Boyd continues to keep a diary of what God reveals to him regarding the world, Relationship to the Father and his place within it all. The rainforest provides the solitude that continues to feed his thoughts, inspiration, gratitude and soul.

Both he and his wife are active in helping other alcoholics to achieve sobriety. They attend 12-step meetings as often as possible and welcome *any* opportunity to share their experience, strength and hope with those who still suffer.

Statistics show that regardless of *who* a person is or *what* they may feel 'called' to do in life, 2-in-10 who consume alcohol (*to any degree; at any level*) are not "normal" drinkers and will eventually develop a problem with alcohol beyond their ability to resolve on their own. Even with abundant resources now available to alcoholics, only 3-in-100 will ever achieve lasting sobriety. Of the remaining 97, most will go on to the 'bitter end', relegated to asylums, incarcerations and, ultimately, death.

www.thealcoholicmissionary.com

> **"Remember that we deal with alcohol – cunning, baffling, powerful! Without help it is too much for us. But there is One who has all Power – that One is God. May you find Him NOW!"** (*Page 58; The Big Book of Alcoholics Anonymous; 4th Edition)

www.ingramcontent.com/pod-product-compliance
Lightning Source LLC
Chambersburg PA
CBHW051648040426
42446CB00009B/1026